THE 1986 DEFENSE BUDGET

STUDIES IN DEFENSE POLICY

THE 1986 DEFENSE BUDGET

William W. Kaufmann

THE BROOKINGS INSTITUTION
Washington, D.C.

THE BROOKINGS INSTITUTION is an independent organization devoted to nonpartisan research, education, and publication in economics, government, foreign policy, and the social sciences generally. Its principal purposes are to aid in the development of sound public policies and to promote public understanding of issues of national importance.

The Institution was founded on December 8, 1927, to merge the activities of the Institute for Government Research, founded in 1916, the Institute of Economics, founded in 1922, and the Robert Brookings Graduate School of Economics and Government, founded in 1924.

The Board of Trustees is responsible for the general administration of the Institution, while the immediate direction of the policies, program, and staff is vested in the President, assisted by an advisory committee of the officers and staff. The by-laws of the Institution state: "It is the function of the Trustees to make possible the conduct of scientific research, and publication, under the most favorable conditions, and to safeguard the independence of the research staff in the pursuit of their studies and in the publication of the results of such studies. It is not a part of their function to determine, control, or influence the conduct of particular investigations or the conclusions reached."

The President bears final responsibility for the decision to publish a manuscript as a Brookings book. In reaching his judgment on the competence, accuracy, and objectivity of each study, the President is advised by the director of the appropriate research program and weighs the views of a panel of expert outside readers who report to him in confidence on the quality of the work. Publication of a work signifies that it is deemed a competent treatment worthy of public consideration but does not imply endorsement of conclusions or recommendations.

The Institution maintains its position of neutrality on issues of public policy in order to safeguard the intellectual freedom of the staff. Hence interpretations or conclusions in Brookings publications should be understood to be solely those of the authors and should not be attributed to the Institution, to its trustees, officers, or other staff members, or to the organizations that support its research.

FOREWORD

MOST of the decisions reflected in the annual defense budget have been made in prior years. Unless these decisions are periodically reviewed and challenged, the budgetary changes that can realistically be expected in any given year are bound to be limited. Because such reviews are complex and often divisive, Congress and public debate tend to focus on marginal adjustments to administration proposals. The threats to U.S. security, the basic force structure, and the overall composition of the defense effort rarely come under review.

Under most conditions, the incremental approach to defense planning may be acceptable as well as politically realistic. However, a number of factors now warrant a more fundamental review. Unusually large increases in the defense budget over the past four years, especially in defense investment, and unusually large federal deficits make the currently projected path of the defense effort difficult if not impossible to follow. At some point major changes of direction will be irresistible. If not anticipated and intelligently designed, the changes are likely to damage the defense effort. For these reasons, it is important to identify the major defense issues and encourage public debate. That is the purpose of this volume.

Funding for this study was provided in part by the Ford Foundation under a grant supporting national security studies at Brookings. The views expressed are those of the author and should not be ascribed to the Ford Foundation or to the trustees, officers, or other staff members of the Brookings Institution.

BRUCE K. MACLAURY
President

March 1985
Washington, D.C.

THE 1986 DEFENSE BUDGET

William W. Kaufmann

PRESIDENT Reagan, like the Duke of Wellington after Waterloo, has ample reason to believe that "Nothing except a battle lost can be half so melancholy as a battle won." The president has gained a famous victory over his Democratic challenger, but he has incurred heavy costs in the process. Federal deficits have climbed to stunning levels, with adverse effects on real interest rates, economic growth, and the U.S. balance of payments. Moreover, the deficits will continue to grow as far as the eye can see unless stern action is taken soon to balance the government's books.

Whatever remedies the president may recommend to improve the nation's fiscal health, other economizers are bound to make the defense budget and five-year program a target for major savings in current and future outlays. That this should be the case is understandable. Defense outlays constituted 29 percent of total federal spending in fiscal year 1984 and account for 76 percent of all goods and services purchased by the federal government. While total federal spending from fiscal 1980 through 1984 has grown in real terms by 13 percent, real defense outlays have expanded by 26 percent. At the outset of the Reagan administration these outlays took 5.2 percent of the nation's gross national product; that share is now 6.5 percent of a larger GNP.

Growth and size alone, however, do not explain why defense programs should be a target for reductions or slower growth in the future. Many members of Congress believe that as a matter of equity or expediency, if domestic programs are to be cut, defense should be cut as well. In

The author thanks Richard K. Betts, Colonel John Buckelew, Bruce K. MacLaury, Michael K. MccGwire, Joseph A. Pechman, and John D. Steinbruner for their comments, Alan G. Hoden and Lisa B. Mages for assistance in verifying the factual data, and Kathryn Ho for working on the manuscript above and beyond the call of duty.

1

addition, as a result of overpriced hammers and coffee pots, new spare parts prematurely sold as surplus, and contracting practices designed seemingly for the convenience of the producers rather than for the protection of the public, members of Congress may suspect that defense already has at its disposal more resources than it knows how to manage. And this suspicion is reinforced by the rapidly changing rationale given by the administration for its programs and their growth.

These attitudes, doubts, and reservations, whatever their merits, do not lead automatically to conclusions about the specific amounts of budget authority or outlays that could be cut from defense in 1986 (the coming fiscal year), in the out years (1987–90), or even in prior fiscal years by means of congressional rescissions. Consequently, unless budget surgery is to be arbitrary and possibly damaging to the patient, two questions need to be answered. What defense capabilities are required to ensure low risk to U.S. security, and what are their costs? How do past and current defense plans and programs mesh with these requirements?

Defense Requirements and Risk

Each year through their Joint Strategic Planning Document, the Joint Chiefs of Staff provide an estimate of the "minimum-risk" capabilities required to maintain U.S. security. These capabilities are used as the benchmark against which to measure the adequacy of current plans and programs. As might be expected, a gap invariably exists between what the Joint Chiefs regard as required and what the president and the secretary of defense consider to be politically and fiscally feasible. One way to deal with the gap is to challenge the merits of the proposed minimum-risk force (an example of which is shown in table 1) and discard it as a benchmark. Another way is to use the gap as the reason for continuing to increase the defense budget. Even when this is done, however, the gap never seems to disappear.

This inability to close the gap should come as no surprise. Unhampered by fiscal restraints, the concept of the minimum-risk force is a collection of the Holy Grails sought by each of the services and a device to ensure that no matter how compliant the civilian leadership of the Pentagon, the responsibility for any future failures in the field will not fall on the Joint Chiefs of Staff. To say this, however, is not to deny that the idea

Table 1. Minimum-Risk Forces Projected by the Joint Chiefs of Staff, Fiscal Year 1991

Forces	Active duty	Reserve
Army divisions	25	8
Aircraft carrier battle groups	22	...
Marine amphibious forces	4	1
Air Force tactical fighter wings	38	19
Intercontinental lift aircraft	632	...
Intratheater lift aircraft	458	302
Fleet ballistic missile submarines	44	...
Strategic bombers	483	...
Intercontinental ballistic missiles	1,254	...

Source: *Armed Forces Journal International*, vol. 119 (August 1982), p. 38.

of a minimum-risk force has merit. Provided it is the product of study rather than stapling machines, it can give key policymakers a sense of the relationship among budgets, forces, and the probability of reaching objectives.

The concept of the minimum-risk force can also help dispel a frequently repeated myth that capabilities must match commitments and that if they do not, either the capabilities or the commitments must undergo some unspecified adjustment. Admittedly, the effort to relate capabilities to commitments is a difficult one, depending as it does on the nature and importance of the commitment, available allied forces, mobility, logistics, and what a potential enemy is able to do. But there is always some probability that a given set of capabilities at a given cost will be able to fulfill the commitments. Policymakers need to understand, therefore, that a wide range of choice lies between a carefully crafted minimum-risk force that appears to guarantee success and one that would be very likely to fail. Rather than argue about cutting commitments to fit capabilities or increasing capabilities to satisfy commitments, they should focus on how much they are willing to pay to reduce the risk, and at what point they run into rapidly diminishing returns. If they dislike high risks and low probabilities, they can then choose explicitly to assume the substantial premiums associated with improved coverage (premiums that the United States and its allies can easily afford to pay). Talk about requirements and about tailoring commitments to capabilities (or vice versa) simply conceals these choices.

The description of a minimum-risk force thus may be a necessary condition of sound military advice, but it is hardly sufficient, particularly when it is unaccompanied by costs. Even though planning staffs may fear that civilian policymakers, if offered a range of costs, capabilities, and risks, will always choose low costs and high risks, the danger of insisting that the minimum-risk force is the only option is equally great. For in the process of demanding the unattainable best (if it really is that), the attainable good may be excluded.

If the issue seems abstract and without operational implications, several considerations should be recalled. First, the United States is committed either by formal treaty or by presidential declaration and executive agreement to come to the aid of more than forty nations in the Western Hemisphere, Europe, the Middle East, Southwest Asia, and the Far East. Second, nuclear forces aside, the United States deploys only twenty active-duty divisions, twenty-nine land-based fighter-attack wings of aircraft, and a navy of 545 ships by the current rules of counting. On top of that apparent disparity between commitments and capabilities, alarm (recently muted) has been expressed about a window of strategic nuclear vulnerability and about the inability of the United States and its allies to withstand a major conventional attack by the Warsaw Pact in central Europe without resorting to the tactical use of nuclear weapons (where the Warsaw Pact is also alleged to have superiority). Some observers are also concerned about the apparent nakedness of the Middle East oil states to a Soviet invasion through Iran, about the buildup of North Korean forces along the demilitarized zone in Korea, about communist infiltration of Central America, and about the U.S. Navy's supposed loss of its necessary (but undefined) margin of superiority over the Soviet fleet. Indeed, if the Reagan administration is to be believed, the military situation has been desperately unfavorable for some time. Because U.S. capabilities have changed very little during the past four years, despite congressional appropriations of nearly $900 billion for defense, the situation must still be desperate.

But just how desperate is it? What resources invested in which areas will make how much difference? Do policymakers have no choice between existing capabilities and the minimum-risk force, or is there an intermediate military posture that lowers the risk but does so without breaking the bank? Obviously such a point must exist because the pessimism about the military situation is actually an implicit admission that the probability of successfully meeting commitments is low but not zero (why, otherwise, has World War III not begun?). Presumably that probability can be raised with an increase of resources.

The Threat

It is important to realize that much of the administration's original pessimism about fulfilling commitments rested on a rather simple comparison of what the United States and the Soviet Union are supposed to be spending on defense. As the secretary of defense expressed it, while U.S. defenses suffered from a decade or more of neglect, the USSR embarked on the biggest military buildup in modern history. These diverging trends had inevitably led to a host of U.S. vulnerabilities and the rising danger of military defeat or political collapse in the face of Soviet pressure. Thus the rate at which resources were pumped into defense needed to be raised by substantially more than the 5 percent a year real growth proposed by the Carter administration in its farewell five-year plan for fiscal 1982–86.

It is possible to question whether inputs of dollars or rubles rather than outputs such as forces and their performance are the most appropriate way to measure the relative power of two great nations with differing concerns and objectives. But in any event the administration did not get the comparison quite right. Whether U.S. defense capabilities actually suffered a decade or more of neglect is at least arguable considering that the services received a great deal of new equipment and substantial stocks of munitions as a result of the war in Vietnam, that $185 billion was spent on procurement alone from fiscal 1974 through fiscal 1980, that most of the improvements claimed for the defense establishment during the last four years are the result of decisions made during the Ford and Carter presidencies, and that the NATO nations as a whole have consistently spent more on defense than the Warsaw Pact members. More important, the precise size and direction of the Soviet buildup has become a matter of some doubt. Data about the resources actually committed to defense by the USSR are relatively sparse, and analysts have difficulty equating these data with U.S. defense expenditures. As a consequence, the Central Intelligence Agency uses a methodology that tries to determine what it would cost to buy the Soviet military program in the U.S. economy—that is, paying U.S. prices for the goods and services, materiel and men, provided to the Soviet defense establishment. While this methodology has its drawbacks (as the CIA is the first to acknowledge), its results are extensively used and provide the basis for the claim that Soviet defense spending has grown by 4 percent a year in real terms since 1964, that the total each year now exceeds that of the United States by about 50 percent (with pensions excluded on both sides), and that Soviet defense investments—which consist of military procurement, research, development, test, and evaluation and of construction—are greater by 80 to 90 percent.[1]

Assuming for the moment that these claims are correct, what do they demonstrate? At a minimum, it is disconcerting to contend with a potential adversary who, year in and year out, commits an estimated 13 to 14 percent of his GNP to military pursuits, and it is hardly prudent to let such an effort proceed without response from the United States and its allies. But the design of the response needs to take into account more than the magnitude of the Soviet effort. For example, the steady increases associated with Brezhnev's accession to power were probably intended to compensate for the reductions imposed by Khrushchev on Soviet ground forces and for his efforts to get by with a relatively modest deployment of strategic nuclear forces. Under Brezhnev, and even under Khrushchev, concern about future relations with China led to a buildup of Soviet nuclear and conventional forces in the Far East that accounted for about 25 percent of the increase in dollar-computed expenditures. It is also worth noting that some American defense analysts consider real increases of 3 to 4 percent a year in the defense budget as necessary to allow for the systematic modernization of the U.S. forces. Conceivably Soviet military planners were more successful than their American counterparts in persuading the Kremlin to budget on that basis. Quite possibly, growth in the defense budget was also tied to growth in the Soviet GNP.

However these rates of growth may be explained, what has been evident for more than a year is that they proved less relentless than the Defense Department claimed. Even the Defense Intelligence Agency has agreed that, measured in the U.S. economy, the rate of growth in Soviet defense spending, while averaging 4 percent a year in real terms until 1974, fell to an annual average of 3 percent between 1974 and 1976, and dropped to 2 percent a year between 1976 and at least 1981. What is more, from 1976 to 1981 (and probably for longer) *investment* did not grow at all in real terms: such increases as did occur went to operating

---

1. *Allocation of Resources in the Soviet Union and China—1984*, Hearings before the Subcommittee on International Trade, Finance, and Security Economics of the Joint Economic Committee, 99 Cong. 1 sess. (Government Printing Office, forthcoming).

and supporting the forces. Presumably an upturn in real investment has occurred since 1983, but whether it has extended beyond the relatively sterile area of strategic and intermediate-range nuclear systems is not yet publicly clear.

Because Soviet spending on defense was already high, as measured by the CIA methodology, too much comfort cannot be drawn from the slowdown in real defense growth and the flatness of spending on investment. As defense spokesmen hasten to point out (but only about the Soviet Union), large defense budgets, even if they do not grow, still permit a substantial modernization of forces. Nonetheless, to the extent that these comparisons are useful—and they at least indicate trends—they suggest that the military balance of power may not have been as unfavorable to the United States and its allies as the administration originally assumed and as the Defense Department continued to proclaim even after the new assessments of the Soviet defense effort began to appear.

Strategic Nuclear Capabilities

Other analyses—assessments of U.S. strategic nuclear forces, for instance—also suggest a stronger military position for the United States. The strategic capabilities inherited by the Reagan administration have changed very little since 1981, and the changes that have occurred were started and funded by the Carter administration. Nonetheless, these forces can still give an impressive account of themselves. Even in the wake of a well-executed Soviet surprise attack directed at U.S. ICBMs, bomber bases, strategic submarine ports, and air defense installations, the inherited capabilities should have nearly an 80 percent probability of delivering more than 3,660 warheads against a wide range of aiming points. Unless the Soviet attack crippled the U.S. command-control system, the president or his designated successor would also have the option of withholding a large part of the surviving warheads, particularly those carried by submarine-launched ballistic missiles (SLBMs), and retaliating only against a subset of the very long target list contained in the basic U.S. war plan. It is difficult in these circumstances to believe that the United States does not continue to have a powerful strategic nuclear deterrent or that a window of vulnerability has existed or is likely to open in the next few years.

Potential Developments

To make this assessment is not to claim that policymakers can confidently count on the U.S. strategic forces to deter anything less than strategic nuclear attacks on the United States and its allies. Nor is it to suggest that the problem of nuclear deterrence has been solved now and forever. The role of strategic nuclear forces has been severely limited by the growth of Soviet strategic capabilities. At the same time, the technology of the offense and the defense has advanced. Ballistic and cruise missiles are growing more accurate and perhaps more reliable, and the degree of accuracy is becoming less dependent on whether the launch platform is stationary or mobile. With the advent of better detection systems, air defenses now have the ability to identify, track, and intercept low-flying bombers with fairly large radiating surfaces (known as their radar cross-section), although stealth technology can be used to reduce these radar cross-sections and lower the probability that newer bombers and cruise missiles will be detected. Advances are also taking place in antiballistic missile (ABM) defenses, and either the United States or the Soviet Union or both may be tempted to deploy the less exotic of these systems as a way of reducing the vulnerability of their ICBMs. Improvements can also be expected in the various devices used to identify and track submarines, but submarines are becoming quieter and thus more difficult to engage.

These developments have already jeopardized the survivability of silo-based ICBMs, although their vulnerability has probably been exaggerated. In the coming years these same developments will undoubtedly complicate the task of penetrating enemy defenses. Hence unless future arms control agreements can forestall them, the competition between the offense and the defense is almost certain to continue and even accelerate as both the United States and the Soviet Union expand their strategic defense initiatives, seek to improve further the yield-to-weight ratio of their warheads, emphasize greater throw weight as a means of carrying more reentry vehicles and decoys, and apply stealth technologies to submarines, bombers, and cruise missiles. Because it seems to take an average of at least five years to conclude a major arms control agreement, even an optimist would probably want to allow the force planners enough freedom to explore, develop, and deploy some of these putative capabilities. The issue facing the policymakers is which ones?

The ability of the United States to deliver warheads to targets in the Soviet Union on a second strike has already eroded somewhat, largely because of the growing vulnerability of the Minuteman ICBM force. If U.S. planners did nothing to modernize the strategic offense, they would have to anticipate a more serious loss of retaliatory power. Within a decade, the survivability of the ICBM force could fall from 20 percent to 5 percent. Despite the dismal performance of Soviet air defenses against Korean airliners, the introduction of a detection capability equivalent to that of the U.S. Airborne Warning and Control System (AWACS) could sharply reduce the probability that large, low-flying bombers such as the B-52H could penetrate to their targets. Even some of the SLBMs could conceivably be threatened. Improved Soviet antisubmarine warfare capabilities might permit attacks on Poseidon submarines carrying the shorter-range C-3 ballistic missile (unless they are retired in the early 1990s), and a widespread deployment of antiballistic missile defenses could reduce the probability that their warheads would penetrate. Although the inherited force could be expected to deliver a substantial number of warheads (table 2) despite the possible improvements in Soviet offensive and defensive capabilities, the probability of their delivery would have fallen dramatically, especially in the case of the ICBMs and the bombers. The country could no longer have high confidence in the retaliatory effectiveness of the strategic offense and hence in its deterrent power.

Fortunately, most of the measures necessary to prevent the further erosion of the U.S. nuclear capability are already in hand. The gradual introduction of the Trident submarine and the deployment of the C-4 (Trident I) missile mean that twelve of the Poseidon and all Trident boats can fire their missiles from stations well beyond the probable range of effective Soviet antisubmarine forces. The C-4, with its increased throw weight and greater ability to carry either a larger number of warheads or more decoys than its predecessors, should also have a higher probability of penetrating any Soviet ABM defenses. With the deployment of the D-5 (Trident II) missile, starting perhaps as early as 1989, not only will more throw weight per missile become available, but for the first time a significant capacity to destroy hard targets will also be deployed in the strategic submarine force. Simultaneously, the bomber force will have an improved ability to penetrate upgraded enemy air defenses, principally because of the deployment of air-launched cruise missiles—first the ALCM-B and then the advanced cruise missile (ACM)—which will also have a significant probability of destroying hard targets. Of course,

Table 2. Estimated Performance of the Day-to-Day Alert Strategic Forces Inherited by the Reagan Administration, Fiscal Year 1985

Item	Warheads Inventory	Warheads Surviving	Alert	Targets and alert weapons assignments — Strategic Hard[b]	Strategic Soft	Peripheral attack[a]	General purpose forces	Energy and logistics	Urban/ industrial	Total
Targets	...	...	...	1,598	752	640	404	500	1,380	5,274
Forces										
550 Minuteman III	1,650	330	297	297	...	...	...	...	...	297
450 Minuteman II	450	90	81	81	...	...	...	...	...	81
304 Poseidon C-3	3,040	1,672	1,505	...	107	18	...	103	1,380	1,505
192 Poseidon C-4	1,344	806	725	...	...	622	...	...	...	725
144 Trident C-4	1,008	605	545	...	...	...	404	141	...	545
145 B-52G	1,160	348	348	...	348	...	...	...	...	348
96 B-52H	768	230	230	...	230	...	...	...	...	230
56 FB-111A	224	67	67	...	67	...	...	...	...	67
Total	9,644	4,148	3,798	378	752	640	404	244	1,380	3,798
Targets damaged	...	...	...	215	498	512	323	195	1,104	2,847
Percent	...	...	...	13	66	80	80	39	80	54

Source: Author's estimates.
a. Soviet medium-range forces targeted against U.S. allies.
b. Includes launch control centers and nuclear storage sites.

cruise missiles would reach those targets hours later than ballistic missiles, but that could be an advantage rather than a disadvantage on a second strike because those few hours might suffice to bring about an end to the exchange.

Assuming that the United States continues the SALT II limit on the deployment of ALCMs (3,360 on 120 bombers), how well would the improved submarine and bomber forces combined with the existing Minuteman ICBMs perform after a Soviet surprise attack? Table 3 indicates that despite an upgraded Soviet offense and defense the SLBMs and ALCMs of the improved force would have a high probability of reaching their targets. Along with the few surviving Minuteman ICBMs, they could be expected to deliver at least 3,100 weapons against a mixture of hard and soft targets with only tactical warning. If the forces were already on a generated alert, which they would probably be during a major Soviet-American confrontation, they could expect to deliver 5,700 weapons.

If the SALT II limitations were abandoned and wide-bodied commercial aircraft were adapted as cruise missile platforms, the number of deliverable weapons could rise still further (table 4). Indeed, with or without SALT a cruise missile carrier would be an inexpensive way to replace the B-52s as and when they reach the end of their useful service lives.

Administration Programs

The capabilities shown in tables 3 and 4 should provide deterrence of a very high order for well beyond a decade and should also put pressure on the Soviet Union to improve strategic stability by reducing its dependence on silo-based ICBMS.[2] The administration, however, has not been content to settle for these achievements. It has fought long, hard, and with considerable success on three fronts to modernize the

---

2. As long as the USSR continues to base its ICBMs in silos and rely heavily on them for its nuclear striking power, it will have to worry (however unrealistically) about the possibility of a U.S. first strike. That in turn will force Soviet leaders to rely on mobile forces, authorize a preemptive strategy, or design launch-on-warning tactics as a way to improve the survivability of their ICBMs. Mobility for these forces will be costly, but it will combine increased survivability with improved stability. Soviet planners, fortunately, seem to recognize the advantages of this choice.

Table 3. Estimated Performance of the Modernized Day-to-Day Alert Strategic Forces under SALT II Limitations on Cruise Missiles, 1992

| | Warheads | | | Targets and alert weapons assignments | | | | | | |
| | | | | Strategic | | | | | | |
Item	Inventory	Surviving	Alert	Hard	Soft	Peripheral attack[a]	General purpose forces	Energy and logistics	Urban/ industrial	Total
Targets	...	...	...	992[b]	752	640	404	500	1,380	4,668
Forces										
416 Minuteman III	1,248	62	56	56	...	...	...	...	...	56
450 Minuteman II	450	23	21	21	...	...	...	...	...	21
304 Poseidon C-3	3,040	1,672[c]	1,505	...	125	...	...	...	1,380	1,505
192 Poseidon C-4	1,344	739[c]	665	...	...	...	404	261	...	665
144 Trident C-4	1,008	605[c]	545	...	...	541	...	4	...	545
144 Trident D-5	1,008	605[c]	545	545	...	...	...	...	...	545
120 B-52G/ALCM	2,400	720	720	351	369	...	...	...	...	720
25 B-52G	200	60	60	...	60	...	...	...	...	60
96 B-52H	768	230	230	...	131	99	...	...	...	230
56 FB-111A	224	67	67	...	67	...	...	...	...	67
Total	11,690	4,783	4,414	973	752	640	404	265	1,380	4,414
Targets damaged	...	...	...	630	560	496	323	212	1,104	3,325
Percent	...	...	...	64	75	78	80	42	80	71

Source: Author's estimates.

a. Soviet medium-range forces targeted against U.S. allies.

b. Does not include 600 Soviet ICBMs assumed to be mobile and not targetable.

c. These are the warheads actually on station in normal peacetime conditions. Perhaps as many as 1,600 more warheads would be on submarines in transit to and from their stations. They could not be targeted and could either be returned to station for use or withheld as a postwar reserve.

Table 4. Estimated Performance of the Modernized Alert Strategic Forces without SALT II Limitations on Cruise Missiles, 1992.

Item	Warheads			Targets and alert weapons assignments						
	Inventory	Surviving	Alert	Strategic Hard[b]	Strategic Soft	Peripheral attack[a]	General purpose forces	Energy and logistics	Urban/industrial	Total
Targets	...	...	...	992[b]	752	640	404	500	1,380	4,668
Forces on day-to-day alert										
550 Minuteman III	1,650	83	75	75	...	...	...	...	...	75
450 Minuteman II	450	23	21	21	...	...	...	...	...	21
304 Poseidon C-3	3,040	1,672	1,505	...	125	...	...	...	1,380	1,505
192 Poseidon C-4	1,344	739	665	...	627	6	38	...	...	665
144 Trident C-4	1,008	605	545	...	...	...	366	173	...	545
144 Trident D-5	1,008	605	545	218	...	...	...	327	...	545
241 B-52/ALCM	4,820	1,446	1,446	896	...	550	...	...	...	1,446
10 cruise missile carriers	280	84	84	...	...	84	...	...	...	84
Total	13,600	5,257	4,886	1,210	752	640	404	500	1,380	4,886
Targets damaged	...	...	...	783	602	512	323	400	1,104	3,724
Percent	...	...	...	79	80	80	80	80	80	80
Forces on Emergency alert										
550 Minuteman III	1,650	83	75	75	...	...	...	...	...	75
450 Minuteman II	450	23	21	21	...	...	...	...	...	21
304 Poseidon C-3	3,040	2,432	2,189	...	...	...	...	...	2,189	2,189
192 Poseidon C-4	1,344	1,075	968	...	64	...	404	500	...	968
144 Trident C-4	1,008	806	726	...	688	...	...	...	38	726
144 Trident D-5	1,008	806	726	726	...	...	...	...	...	726
241 B-52/ALCM	4,820	3,856	3,856	2,048	752	1,056	...	...	...	3,856
10 cruise missile carriers	280	224	224	...	...	224	...	...	...	224
Total	13,600	9,305	8,785	2,870	1,504	1,280	404	500	2,227	8,785
Targets damaged	...	...	...	962	722	614	323	400	1,239	4,260
Percent	...	...	...	97	96	96	80	80	90	91

Source: Author's estimates.
a. Soviet medium-range forces targeted against U.S. allies.
b. Does not include 600 Soviet ICBMs assumed to be mobile and not targetable.

strategic forces it inherited and to expand the repertory of strategies these forces could execute.

On the first front the administration has argued for retaining an upgraded version of the strategic offensive triad, lobbied vigorously for deploying the MX missile despite the failure to find a highly survivable basing mode for it, and, in response to congressional pressure and the advocacy of the Scowcroft Commission, launched the development of a small ICBM. This missile would presumably (but not necessarily) be armed with a single warhead and would depend for survival on its ability to be moved rapidly by a hardened vehicle (frequently referred to as Armadillo). It would be something like a land-based submarine but without a submarine's peacetime operating area or its ability to stay mobile and concealed for weeks at a time.

On the second front the administration has insisted on retaining the tradition of the manned penetrating bomber in addition to cruise missiles. It has revived the B-1B for deployment in the late 1980s and continued development of the stealth or advanced-technology bomber for deployment in the 1990s.

On the third front the administration has modernized the continental air defenses of the United States and advocated a major expansion of what for more than twenty years has been the façade of a civil defense program. More important, it has instituted what is now known as the strategic defense initiative. This program, which is scheduled to grow rapidly during the coming years, combines development of the more familiar techniques for attempting to intercept and destroy ballistic missile reentry vehicles with research into methods of using directed energy devices such as lasers and particle beam generators to intercept ballistic missiles soon after their launch and before they have deployed multiple independently targetable reentry vehicles (MIRVs) and decoys.

Since the Reagan administration has been in office, the Defense Department has provided about $40 billion for the main programs in these three areas. Between fiscal 1985 and 1989 it hopes to fund them for at least another $80 billion. This amount is over and above the cost of the modernized inherited force that already provides a strong deterrent. It is by no means clear that most of that premium is worth paying.

Several of the programs for the strategic offense are based primarily on the presumed need to strengthen the strategic triad. In the abstract there is merit to the case. Although the triad did not come about by holy writ, it has conferred a number of advantages on the United States in complicating a Soviet attack, in discouraging the Kremlin from deploying even more elaborate defenses than it has already, and in minimizing the kind of shock that occurred when, in the late 1950s, Americans feared that only a few hundred Soviet missiles could destroy the entire Strategic Air Command, then only a uniad rather than a triad.

The ICBM Problem

The ICBM leg of the triad has proved particularly valuable for more than twenty years because of its high survivability in silos, the relative ease with which it could be controlled, the higher accuracy of missiles fired from precisely known locations, and its modest investment and operating costs compared with those of bombers and SLBMs. None of this, however, argues that some percentage of the ICBM warheads must be made survivable regardless of the cost. Nor can past benefits possibly justify spending some $30 billion for 100 MX missiles with 1,000 warheads when no more than 5 missiles and 50 warheads could be expected to survive an enemy attack. The benefits seem particularly incommensurate with the costs when it is recalled that the highly survivable and accurate D-5 (Trident II) missile will be deployed several years after the date proposed for the MX.

The argument has been made and will be heard frequently in the months to come that whatever its basing problems, MX cannot be canceled because it has become a major bargaining chip in the negotiations for arms control with the Soviet Union. But that is surely a perversion of the legitimate case for bargaining chips. A weapon can become a serious bargaining chip only when it has demonstrated military value and would definitely be deployed short of a compensatory concession by the USSR. Considering the opposition to it and its doubtful military value because of its vulnerability, the MX hardly qualifies. In any event, why would the Soviets pay a major price for the cancellation of the MX when they would still have to deal with the threat of the D-5 and cruise missiles?

The small ICBM (SICBM or Midgetman) has been proposed as a substitute for the Minuteman and the MX and as a way of improving strategic stability. Because the SICBM would weigh far less than the MX—about 35,000 pounds compared to 190,000 pounds—it could be made truly mobile and allegedly more survivable. And because it would carry only one warhead instead of the ten in the MX and the three in the Minuteman III (of which there are 550) it would constitute a less tempting target for a Soviet preemptive strike. The merit of these arguments, however, depends critically on the size of the area in which the SICBM would be located (before and after warning, if any), and on the number and yield of the weapons the Soviets could allocate to cover that area with sufficient blast overpressure to destroy the system.

The problem of the mobile missile can be compared to that of a tank. It can be heavily armored, which would limit speed and range, or it can be lightly armored and have greater speed and range. The choice of design, always difficult, is complicated further by the power of nuclear weapons. If they are airburst, they can cover many square miles with overpressures of up to 150 psi. Unless the SICBM transporter can be made both speedy and resistant to quite high overpressures or unless it can operate regularly in a very large area, an enemy can destroy it by blanketing the area rather than by attacking the individual missiles. Table 5 shows the number of weapons required to destroy whatever number of SICBMs might be deployed as a function of the operating area of the SICBMs, the hardness of their transporters, and the yields of the nuclear weapons detonated in the attack. Even for extensive areas and for transporters capable of withstanding overpressures up to 50 psi, a barrage attack would be feasible, given the ICBM throw weight the Soviets already deploy. Furthermore, if 1,000 SICBMs were within the potential operating areas, the Soviets would have a strong incentive to develop the specific capability to destroy them.

Solutions to the vulnerability of land-based ballistic missiles may, of course, be found. Arms control might possibly constrain throw weight enough to prevent effective barrage attacks, and both sides might choose mobility for their future ICBMs. Research on advanced basing modes needs to continue. But as matters now stand, neither the MX nor the SICBM promises to give a high-confidence solution to the basing problem without a much more serious reduction in Soviet throw weight than can be anticipated from any arms control agreement in the foreseeable future. Moreover, given the arrival of the D-5 SLBM and the air-launched cruise missile with their potential for destroying hard targets, the argument that MX or SICBM is needed to threaten Soviet silos (and to force Soviet planners to wrestle with the basing problem as well) is no longer persuasive. Finally, to the extent that the existence of the ICBMs complicates an enemy's attack and contributes to the survivability of

Table 5. Number of Enemy Weapons Required to Cover SICBM Operating Area under Varying Conditions[a]

	Number of enemy weapons by yield (mt)			
Conditions	*0.4*	*0.7*	*1.0*	*5.0*
28-minute warning; transporter operating area 30,788 sq. mi.				
Hardness of SICBM transporter (psi)				
20	5,110	3,518	2,774	949
40	10,220	7,037	5,548	1,897
50	12,733	8,796	6,934	2,372
20-minute warning; transporter operating area 15,708 sq. mi.				
Hardness of SICBM transporter (psi)				
20	2,607	1,795	1,415	484
40	5,214	3,590	2,831	968
50	6,517	4,448	3,533	1,210
14-minute warning; transporter operating area 7,700 sq. mi.				
Hardness of SICBM transporter (psi)				
20	1,278	880	694	237
40	2,556	1,760	1,388	474
50	3,194	2,200	1,734	593
7-minute warning; transporter operating area 1,925 sq. mi.				
Hardness of SICBM transporter (psi)				
20	320	220	173	59
40	639	440	347	119
50	799	550	434	148

Source: Author's estimates.

a. Assumes SICBM missile transporter speed of 30 mph. The operating area is assumed to be a function of the speed of the SICBM transporter and the warning time received. The number of weapons required by the enemy to destroy the SICBM force is assumed to be a function of the size of the operating area, the hardness of the missile transporter, and the yield of the weapon used by the enemy.

alert bombers, some or all of the Minuteman force can continue to perform that function and do so at a significantly lower cost than the MX or SICBM. Both programs could be canceled or deferred without any loss of U.S. retaliatory capability.

The Future of Bombers

The case for the B-1B and even the advanced-technology (stealth) bomber is equally difficult to make. Traditionally, advocates of the manned penetrating bomber have justified it for four reasons. First, it is the one strategic system that is confidently known to work because, unlike missiles, it can be and is operated on a daily basis. Second, the alert part of the bomber force (currently 30 percent of the total) can be launched on warning. Not only is it a survivable system, but it is also controllable: it can be recalled after launch. Third, because it has a crew, the aircraft has unique operating flexibility. It can perform reconnaissance and assess bomb damage, and it can also attack targets of opportunity as it roams over enemy territory. Finally, some portion of the force can always be modified and used for conventional bombing campaigns, as SAC B-52s were in the war in Vietnam.

However emollient these arguments may seem, there is a fly in each of the ointments. Bombers are regularly flown, but because they cannot be tested directly against enemy defenses, some uncertainty must always exist about their ability to reach targets, although cruise missiles launched at a distance from these defenses considerably reduce this uncertainty (or will when they improve in reliability) because of their large numbers and small size. Furthermore, the cruise missile married to a manned airborne launch-platform is no more nor less controllable than the manned penetrator. Aircraft have to be launched on warning because it is so difficult to protect them on the ground. Once launched, they are recallable and would automatically return to base if not specifically ordered to go beyond a certain point (their positive control line) and proceed to their targets. After these orders are given, the probability is very high that a large raid involving many hundreds of weapons would take place. Indeed, with or without cruise missiles, bombers make nearly certain that a U.S. second strike will be a heavy one. Accordingly, it is essential that the targets for the second strike, and for the bombers as well as the missiles, be chosen with great care in advance of a mission. The argument that bombers armed with nuclear weapons will be able to hunt for and attack targets of opportunity is a romantic relic of World War II and totally out of keeping with current war plans.

Finally, as to whether the B-1B and the stealth bombers, presumably to be acquired in relatively small numbers and at very high cost, will ever be used for conventional missions, much will undoubtedly depend on the circumstances. But as long as B-52s can fly, it seems unlikely that either the B-1B or the stealth bomber would be withdrawn from its nuclear assignment for this purpose. Admittedly, the B-52s now remaining in the strategic bomber force are chronologically ancient as aircraft go. But they have undergone considerable rebuilding and refitting. The Air Force has programmed $1 billion to improve the penetration capabilities of some and another $2 billion to modify others to carry cruise missiles. Consequently, chances are good that they will remain a part of the strategic inventory until at least the end of this decade. Between now and the early 1990s, the B-52Hs—which should do well against Soviet defenses until such time as a true Soviet AWACS is deployed in significant numbers—can hedge against uncertain reliability on the part of cruise missiles. Thereafter, it would seem logical to rely on cruise missiles to penetrate improved Soviet defenses and to replace the B-52s with an aircraft specifically designed as a missile platform.

Active Defenses

Although SLBMs and cruise missiles ensure a powerful offense in the future, do they preclude a role in strategic nuclear deterrence for active and passive defenses? Like others before him, the president has envisioned a leakproof defense against ballistic missiles that would replace the brutal threat of the offense as the road to peace and safety in the twenty-first century. Such a vision should not be denigrated, and we should not deny the desirability of exploring the various technologies that might lead to that end. The president's strategic defense initiative, in fact, is largely a repackaging and acceleration of programs previous administrations insitituted to respond to Soviet efforts in this exotic realm and to explore the implications of the new technologies for the offense as well as the defense. What has already become evident, however, is that a perfect defense against ballistic missiles is not likely for the foreseeable future. What is worse, the effort to achieve it will almost certainly stimulate opposing planners to demand quite feasible additions of throw weight and reentry vehicles and decoys to ensure continued coverage of U.S. targets. The cost of the initial defensive effort combined with the cost of the subsequent competition between offense and defense could soon mount to staggering proportions. Agreements severely restricting the number and size of ballistic missiles might alleviate the demands on the defense, but they would undoubtedly have to entail greater reductions than are currently deemed feasible. Furthermore, however remote the possibility of a leakproof defense against ballistic missiles, the effort to achieve it is bound to increase the investment in bombers and the proliferation of cruise missiles, neither of which is affected by a defense against ballistic missiles. And experience with defenses against bombers and cruise missiles is not encouraging. These vehicles, especially when aided by stealth technologies, probably cannot be prevented from penetrating in large numbers to their targets. Although in an era of rapid technological change, planners never should say never, they also need to recognize that despite the improving ability to intercept offensive weapons, the offense is likely to retain a significant cost advantage for at least several more decades and thus is likely to nullify any advances in the defense.

To abandon the president's goal of a leakproof defense is by no means to end the argument for pressing ahead with the strategic defense initiative and improved air defenses against bombers and cruise missiles. A somewhat less demanding goal than total protection is what became known in the 1960s as damage limitation. It was already becoming evident by then that a disarming attack, whether on a first or second strike, would be impossible with the offense alone, at least against diversified and well-protected forces. Planners therefore sought a substitute in the form of a combined offense and defense. The offense would eliminate as many of the enemy's warheads on the ground as possible, active defenses would intercept a large percentage of those that were then fired, and civil defense would mitigate at least the effects of radioactive fallout from those that got through and detonated. This combination of capabilities is bound to be very expensive. However, none of the systems has to work perfectly in order to limit damage to a level deemed acceptable—often defined as 4 percent of the total population in the case of the USSR. Accordingly, a strategy of damage limitation can be used to justify an ABM system even though it may be far less than leakproof.

Although damage limitation was found wanting and was abandoned by U.S. policymakers in the late 1960s, Soviet planners may have picked it up. Whatever the case, the Soviet Union now has ballistic missiles with improved capabilities for destroying hard targets, a large civil defense program, upgraded air defenses, and increasingly sophisticated ABM defenses. Modernization of the ABM system deployed near Moscow is already under way. Whether independently or in mimicry, the Reagan administration is attempting to institute or accelerate comparable programs.

Despite all this activity, for which the Kremlin bears a heavy burden of responsibility, the feasibility of achieving an effective ability to limit damage to acceptable levels remains in doubt. The deployment of large SLBM forces on both sides makes certain that even if an attack were able to eliminate all opposing ICBMs and bombers, many warheads would still survive and be ready for retaliation. Supposing a modern U.S. ABM system could destroy 75 percent of 4,000 Soviet reentry vehicles, 1,000 warheads would still get through. If they were aimed at cities, detonation would kill at least 110 million people immediately (48 percent of the U.S. population), and the effects could be far worse. Furthermore, just as the United States is already taking steps to make sure it can penetrate Soviet active defenses, Soviet planners can be expected to do likewise with respect to U.S. active defenses. If both sides proceed with measure and countermeasure, each may be able to cover its original set of targets as before, but at significantly higher cost. This hardly seems a worthwhile investment for either.

Damage limitation may be only a slightly more promising concept than a leakproof defense. But what about the possibility of providing a ballistic missile defense for the ICBM force, especially if future arms control agreements cannot seriously constrain Soviet capabilities for destroying hard targets? Certainly this is the role in which an ABM system is likely to be most effective. Despite the fratricide phenomenon (where a second or third warhead might be neutralized by the explosion of the first), not only might a strong ballistic missile defense force an enemy to allocate more warheads to each targeted silo, but the defense of ICBMs could also be less exacting and more successful than the defense of cities or other large, soft targets. Some near misses and hits could be tolerated against silos, whereas they would not be acceptable when heavily populated areas are the targets. Nonetheless, it is doubtful that this added protection would be worth either the high cost—perhaps $40 billion in investment alone—or the consequences of having opened yet another arena for strategic competition. The doubt becomes even stronger when it is recognized that ICBM warheads are no longer essential to the coverage of a comprehensive target list in the USSR. On balance, the benefits hardly seem commensurate with the costs and risks.

The Role of the Strategic Nuclear Forces

Some future costs may be avoided as a result of arms control agreements, but the history of arms control, which largely consists of ratifying what both sides did or did not want to do, hardly bodes well for any such savings. More important, the alarms and initiatives of the past four years, the stress that arms control negotiations place on the central role of strategic nuclear forces, and the insistence that there be a response to Soviet modernization of its intermediate-range ballistic missile force (but not to the deployment of Backfire bombers or shorter-range missiles) have once again given the strategic nuclear forces far more political significance than is their due. Indeed, herein lies one of the great paradoxes of this transitional era.

What defense planners have discovered after forty years of trying to adapt to the advent of nuclear weapons is that strategic nuclear forces have a vital but extremely limited military role: deterring their use by an opponent. Also evident, though planners would disagree among themselves about the precise implications, is that the nuclear "balance" is not as delicate as it used to be and therefore more difficult to upset than public rhetoric would suggest. Perhaps less appreciated, but almost certainly as true, arms control agreements of the future, as of the past, are likely to affect the development of the strategic nuclear forces only on the margin. To the extent that nuclear weapons are assigned the very limited political weight to which their limited military role entitles them, moderation in the strategic competition (and perhaps the obsolescence of that competition) will follow much more from planning restraint on each side and a recognition that resources invested elsewhere will have a greater military utility and that further additions to the strategic offense and defense are most unlikely to lead to any meaningful advantage. Benign neglect may be the best to be hoped for here as elsewhere.

Yet at the very time when nuclear weapons are finally being put into true military perspective, the propensity grows to use them for political purposes and to make them the measure of international power and status. Thus the insistence on nothing less than some form of numerical equality in Soviet-American arms control negotiations, however meaningless that particular form of equality may be. Thus the deployment of Pershing II and ground-launched cruise missiles, however great their cost and dubious their military worth. Thus the eagerness of the media to exploit nuclear issues and the inclination of bureaucrats in search of headlines to emphasize those issues beyond their intrinsic importance. Parkinson would recognize the process.

Now as in the past the argument will be made that perceptions are what count in international relations and that because perceptions about the nuclear balance will determine the behavior of friends and foes alike, they must be addressed on their own terms no matter how far they may be removed from the realities of power. Some leaders, however, seem more perceptive than others. Neither Kim il Sung nor Ho Chi Minh was much impressed by U.S. nuclear might, and Mao Zedong defied the Soviet Union despite its manifest nuclear superiority. For those who are more gullible, it is certainly within the power of U.S. statesmen to explain convincingly how limited is the role of nuclear weapons for military and hence for political purposes. And it is certainly cheaper to bring these perceptions into line with reality than to continue the fruitless and costly competition.

Tactical Nuclear Capabilities and Needs

A first step toward greater realism is to question the strategic initiatives of the last four years. A second step, though of less budgetary significance, is to dispel the myths that envelop U.S. tactical nuclear capabilities. These capabilities are increasingly described as weapons of penultimate resort. Even so, they are seen to differ from the strategic forces in that they can achieve traditional military objectives and therefore could restore U.S. and allied fortunes in the event of a reversal in a conventional conflict.

Both propositions might have been true forty years ago when the United States had a monopoly on the tactical use of nuclear weapons, but they lack any serious merit under present conditions. Despite efforts by the Army to reduce the yield of nuclear weapons and to postulate major limitations on their use, nuclear explosives are so powerful and so numerous that traditional Army organizations and operational practices simply cannot be adapted to them. In particular, the notion that ground forces will be able to conduct traditional campaigns of fire and maneuver, advance and retreat, breakthrough and encirclement, and that organizations will be able to retain their coherence, discipline, and control in a nuclear environment boggles the imagination, however appealing the notion may seem to U.S. and Soviet military planners. A more likely eventuality is that any tactical use of nuclear weapons would result in such confusion and panic among both belligerents that chaos would ensue. In principle, such an outcome might be seen as favorable to the United States and its allies. But even if a small-scale use of nuclear weapons caused all the belligerents to collapse, it would start a tidal wave of political consequences, none of which would necessarily favor

Table 6. Estimated Low-Risk Tactical Nuclear Capabilities in Europe under Conditions of Emergency Alert, 1985

		Targets in Eastern Europe and weapons assignments				
Item	Alert weapons	Main airfields	Logistic choke-points	Command and storage bunkers	Troop targets[a]	Total
Targets	...	72	191	162	1,088	1,513
Forces						
480 Submarine-based Tomahawk	384	31	191	162	...	384
116 Ground-launched cruise missiles	104	41	...	...	63	104
108 Pershing II missiles	97	72	...	...	25	97
72 Pershing I missiles (German)	65	...	...	...	65	65
36 Lance missiles	32	...	...	...	32	32
61 Lance missiles (allied)	55	...	...	...	55	55
42 Pluton missiles (French)	38	...	...	...	38	38
Total	775	144	191	162	278	775
Targets damaged	...	69	153	130	222	574
Percent	...	96	80	80	97	88

Source: Author's estimates.
a. As many as 1,088 battalion-sized targets are assumed to exist along a front of 750 kilometers. A blanketing attack covering the entire front with blast effects of 10 psi would require 229 airburst, 50-kiloton weapons.

the United States. And even if shock and chaos were the dominant immediate effects of a first use of nuclear weapons, action would probably be followed by reaction, resulting in a rapid escalation of the exchange and disastrous damage to all belligerents. Moreover, the United States and its allies could find themselves losing militarily in the resulting exchange even more rapidly and with even more horrendous consequences than if they had never used the weapons in the first place. It is no longer realistic, in any event, to pretend that the decision to use nuclear weapons would be taken without much consultation, agony, and delay or that the enemy could not preempt the decision.

Prudent planning in these circumstances would seem to call not for more nuclear bombs and shells or a modernized inventory of enhanced radiation weapons (even though militarily they may be preferable to their predecessors) but for a redesign of the entire capability. Many existing launchers are vulnerable to conventional as well as nuclear attack. Equally disconcerting, most of the aircraft and artillery that would be used to deliver nuclear bombs and shells are also first-line conventional delivery systems. Thus any kind of a military alert in a theater such as central Europe is likely to deprive the conventional forces of some of their most valuable assets precisely at the time when they might be most desperately needed. Furthermore, despite the reductions in deployed weapons that have already taken place and those that are still to come, the overseas nuclear stockpiles remain a truncated artifact of the era when these weapons were seen as a more efficient and advantageous way of conducting a traditional military campaign. Rather than perpetuate this obsolete, vulnerable, and dangerous capability, planners should convert it into a short-range copy of the strategic nuclear forces, limited in its deterrent role and with well-defined targets, more survivable launchers, and the ability to cover the target list at least once on a second strike.

What this means as an operational matter is that aircraft and artillery in a theater such as Europe should be relieved of their nuclear missions, that the main nuclear responsibility should be vested in existing mobile missiles, and that targets should be those assets that would materially assist an enemy in an invasion of allied territory. As can be seen from table 6, the number of weapons needed to cover such an array on a second strike would be relatively small compared to the current stockpile of some 6,000 weapons in Europe (soon to be reduced). Yet such a strike, if released all at once, would permit a barrage attack all along the enemy's front as well as the destruction of his main airfields and lines of communication. The enemy would have the power to destroy Western Europe in a first strike, as he has had for many years. However, if he wished to seize Europe intact, NATO could stop his attempt.

Such a capability would be at least the equal of what is now deployed as a deterrent. Even more important, it would constitute far less of a drag on U.S. and allied conventional capabilities. It would also permit the establishment of a separate command and separate alerting procedures that could be activated independently of and, if desired, later than those of the conventional forces. Beyond that, it would be an acknowledgment that these launchers and weapons exist primarily to deter the first use of nuclear weapons by another party and to give national leaders a choice other than no nuclear response or an immediate release of strategic forces. What is needed, in short, is not more resources or more sophisticated weapons but a recognition that tactical nuclear capabilities, like their strategic counterparts, are severely limited as to the role they can play and the missions they can perform.

Conventional Capabilities

Logic suggests that after forty years of an age that has been proclaimed as nuclear, the real coin of the military realm remains conventional capabilities. Not only are conventional forces the only usable form of military power, as events since 1945 have so strongly underlined, they are also the kind of power in which the United States and its allies have the greatest comparative advantage. Europe alone outruns its prospective enemies in available manpower, industrial output, and technical skills. Nuclear weapons are the great levelers; conventional weapons are what really test a nation's resources of capital, labor, innovation, and determination. The United States and its allies can well afford to acknowledge these realities. Despite certain deficiencies, their conventional strength relative to that of the Soviet Union and its reluctant satellites is much greater than is generally conceded.

Both the administration and the Joint Chiefs of Staff tacitly accept this assessment. Even the minimum-risk force would not require a radical expansion of current active duty and reserve components of the conventional forces except in some marginal respects (as in the number

Table 7. Goals for the Size of Conventional Forces, Fiscal Years 1985, 1989, and 1991

	Secretary of defense				Joint Chiefs of Staff	
	1985		1989		1991	
Forces	Active	Reserve	Active	Reserve	Active	Reserve
Army divisions	17	9	18	10	25	8
Marine amphibious forces	3	1	3	1	4	1
Aircraft carrier battle groups	13	. . .	15	. . .	22	. . .
Air Force tactical fighter wings	26	14	28	15	38	19
Intercontinental lift aircraft	339	. . .	347	. . .	632	. . .
Intratheater lift aircraft	216	302	218	302	458	302

Source: *Department of Defense Annual Report to the Congress, Fiscal Year 1985*, p. 287; *Armed Forces Journal International*, vol. 119 (August 1982), p. 38; and author's estimates.

of carrier battle groups), and as indicated in table 7, the administration's goals are more modest still.

The Administration View

The Defense Department has indicated during the last four years that it has a new way of looking at the conventional forces. The department allegedly rejects specific contingencies for the purpose of assessing and planning these forces; it has spilled a certain amount of rhetoric about the need to prepare for a worldwide conventional war, as though it could be defined separately from specific threats and theaters of conflict; it even talks about the importance of preparing for a war of indefinite duration. As a practical matter, however, the Reagan administration has behaved very much like its immediate predecessors. It has concentrated its ground and tactical air forces on the defense of Germany and Norway, Korea and the oil states of the Persian Gulf area, and on sustaining major conflicts in these theaters for up to sixty days. It has also allocated major resources to the protection of sea lines of communication to these theaters, to what the Navy calls power projection (with carrier battle groups and amphibious forces), and to intercontinental mobility, principally long-range airlift.

Despite these efforts, which consume about 80 percent of total defense outlays (with the nuclear forces accounting for the remaining 20 percent), the administration's prognoses for successful conventional defense and deterrence continue to be pessimistic. One reason is that when it makes a crude comparison of forces, everything on the side of the Soviet Union and its satellites is counted, but only those capabilities known to be in U.S. and allied units are included. Thus Soviet tanks and aircraft parked in storage areas, riverine craft that would be swamped in the open ocean, destroyers in the Caspian Sea, and all those ground and tactical air forces facing China are treated as though they would be available for immediate use against the United States and its allies. No wonder the prospects for a successful defense in one major theater, much less in two, are considered poor.

Even the more sophisticated analyses, which focus on specific theaters, indicate that U.S. and allied forces would not be able to hold out for long against an enemy onslaught, whether by the Warsaw Pact in central Europe, by Soviet units racing down through Iran, or by North Korean armor attacking across the demilitarized zone. Still more discouraging, despite the costly programs of modernization now under way, is that the odds in these theaters do not seem to shift in any significant way. Hence the demand for still more sophisticated aircraft, missiles, and munitions, and for still larger defense budgets. Because of the alleged numerical superiority of opposing forces, technology must deliver extraordinarily high kill rates in every U.S. weapon. And because these weapons are increasingly costly, fewer can be bought, and the kill rates must rise still further.

Perhaps the United States and its allies cannot avoid this vicious circle. However, there are grounds for questioning the prevailing pessimism, the diagnosis of existing deficiencies, and the currently preferred remedies. What needs to be recognized at the outset is that the darkest forecasts are based on contingencies that are usually biased in favor of the enemy. They are the worst of the worst cases. Central Europe, for example, appears so easy to overrun in these projections because the Warsaw Pact is allowed to mobilize and deploy a large number of highly combat-ready units in a very few days, while NATO is permitted very few reinforcements to its forces in West Germany. Yet the evidence suggests strongly that the Warsaw Pact either would need much more time to generate the specified threat or would have to settle for much less combat-ready and reliable forces. In the first eventuality, NATO would be able to deploy many more forces than is generally assumed; in the second, it would face a significantly less awesome attacker. It is worth remembering in this connection that as much as a third of the enemy force would consist of East German, Czech, and Polish units, whose trustworthiness must be in some doubt. Other factors that call Soviet combat effectiveness into doubt, especially early in an attack, include their practice of exercising with older equipment while the new materiel is kept in warehouses; their tradition of training recruits within the operational units, which lowers readiness and causes turbulence as individual soldiers begin and end their terms of service; their dependence on the civilian economy for trucks and the use of the military each autumn to assist in the harvest; and the paucity of maintenance mechanics and spare parts in the forward forces. When these factors are taken into account, NATO has a significantly higher probability of conducting a successful forward defense of West Germany than the pessimists allow.

Improvements Needed

To say this is not to argue that the United States and its allies are entitled to have high confidence in their ability to frustrate an attack in Europe or in other critical theaters. Their main weaknesses and the remedies for them are, however, relatively easy to identify. Most pessimistic projections exaggerate the opposition's ability to mobilize and deploy forces because of the reasonable concern that U.S. and allied leaders will react sluggishly to early and ambiguous indications of enemy activities. To compensate for these anticipated delays, which rule out gradual mobilization and deployment, planners truncate the amount of warning that would be received and establish "requirements" for active-duty units ready to deploy on short notice, for materiel already in position overseas, and for massive airlift capabilities. However, because all three are so costly, and because reserve units and fast sealift cannot compete with them in the short time allegedly available, deployment goals are never reached, and increasingly empty nuclear threats are substituted for realistic and attainable defenses.

It may indeed be the case that political leaders will always procrastinate when confronted with ambiguous warning, although at the outset of the confrontation over Berlin in 1961, President Kennedy deployed U.S. reinforcements to Europe before the Soviet Union made any comparable move. It is also reasonable to expect that these same leaders will be cautious when they are not told about the cost of their caution or the alternatives, and when they have good reason to believe, especially in NATO, that when the deployed forces go on alert they become even more heavily nuclearized than in their peacetime condition.

Is there any way out of this dangerous spiral? A first, obvious, and inexpensive option is to tell U.S. leaders that there will almost always be a great deal of information about the activities of opposing forces and that any major change in the pattern of these activities will be promptly known—perhaps three months before an attack. They should also be advised that even though the warning may be unclear as to the precise consequence of this change, a number of useful alerting and preparatory steps can be taken that save time but do not necessarily signal large-scale mobilization and deployment. A more costly step would be to begin more frequent random exercises related to mobilization and deployment but not tied to any crisis or warning. The redesign of U.S. and allied tactical nuclear capabilities could also reinforce the willingness of political leaders to react more promptly to early signs of opposing mobilization and deployment, because those leaders would no longer have to accept the simultaneous nuclearization of conventional forces and the accompanying loss of valuable conventional capabilities. Finally, because the time for mobilization could be measured in weeks and months instead of a few days, reserve as well as active-duty ground and tactical air units could be deployed, and much greater reliance could be placed on efficient fast sealift than is now intended.

Unfortunately, this is not the direction that the United States and its allies are taking. Because of the assumption that the enemy could attack with so little warning, reserve forces are treated as poor relations and emphasis is placed on such costly expedients as equipment prepositioned in Germany, ships loaded with equipment and supplies on permanent station in the Indian Ocean, and long-range airlift—the only recourse if men and materiel are to be deployed in less than two weeks.

Just as staggering as the cost of this kind of response is the speed and precision with which it must be executed. Yet precisely because of its magnitude—the United States would deploy at least six large divisions and sixty tactical fighter squadrons to Europe alone—and the political repercussions, such a movement almost certainly can never be rehearsed on an adequate scale.

We can, of course, continue with that costly effort. But because time need not be of the essence, and because existing overseas deployments, prepositioned materiel, and airlift provide an adequate hedge against any short-warning attacks that could actually be mounted, other more practicable and less costly options need to be entertained.

To enable the United States to react more effectively to potential military crises will not by itself ensure the high-confidence conventional defenses that are in everyone's interest. It is regrettably easy to imagine a contingency in central Europe during which, over a period of three or four months, the Warsaw Pact could put together a large enough assault force (110 to 120 divisions) to overtax existing NATO forces even if they were fully mobilized and deployed. It takes only a modest further step of the imagination to visualize one or more conflicts occurring in other vital theaters at about the same time, an eventuality that would confront the president with appalling choices, whether he had existing capabilities at his disposal or even the slightly larger forces sought by the administration. The Pentagon has been in the process of adding about 150,000 people to the military establishment, primarily for the Navy and the Air Force, but it would be excessively optimistic to expect a major expansion of the active-duty forces, and particularly of the personnel-intensive ground forces, as long as peacetime conscription is ruled out and the military services must depend on voluntary enlistments that are limited by lower birth rates, rising military standards, and (it is to be hoped) a growing economy.

Fortunately, such an expansion does not seem necessary. The National Guard and the military reserves now consist of more than a million men and women. A significant portion of this reserve, admittedly, is dedicated to rounding out understrength active-duty Army divisions in the event of an emergency and to providing the support forces so necessary in a conventional conflict of any significant duration. Even so, with modern equipment, additional training, and higher standards, more than fourteen divisions and forty-two fighter-attack squadrons could be mustered from the National Guard and reserves and used along with active-duty forces in the event of a greater-than-expected threat in one theater or multiple and more or less simultaneous contingencies.

There is another way to strengthen conventional defenses. On the Korean peninsula, a belt of obstacles and fortifications south of the demilitarized zone makes it difficult for the North Koreans to repeat their early successes of the 1950 war. A similar barrier between the two Germanies would provide a similar hedge against surprise attacks by the

Warsaw Pact and would do much to counter the supposed Soviet superiority in tanks and armored vehicles. Additional close air support for the ground forces, acquired both from the reserves and from trading in the current surplus of Air Force capability for air superiority and interdiction missions deep in Eastern Europe, would also increase confidence that heavy initial attacks on West Germany could be met and defeated.

None of these measures would win popularity contests in the Pentagon. The military services see the National Guard and the reserves as competitors for resources and as threats to their integrity, for if they improve significantly in combat effectiveness and readiness to deploy, yet remain cheaper than active-duty units, Congress will be tempted to reduce active-duty units and increase reserves. The Air Force, still jealous of its independence, resists the idea of supporting the Army and prefers to fight its own war to gain command of the air and destroy enemy lines of communication through interdiction. And technologists in and out of uniform dream of silver bullets that will magically dispose of enemy second- and third-echelon forces, regardless of whether the first echelon, with mundane artillery and tanks, is smashing through U.S. and allied defenses. To produce the necessary changes in priorities will obviously require more than a willingness to fund all requests and to provide a lawyerlike defense of clients regardless of the merits of their claims.

Naval Diversions

Nowhere is the necessity for a new firmness more evident than in the case of the U.S. Navy. In a conventional campaign, especially one of significant duration, naval forces have two vital functions to perform. One is to make sure that the sea lines of communication to the theaters of war remain open, because 95 percent of the tonnage for these theaters is likely to go by sea. The other is to project the power of ground and tactical air forces from sea-based platforms to targets on land in those areas where the much less vulnerable and costly land-based ground and tactical air forces would not be able, at least initially, to operate.

Like the Air Force, but fortified by the traditions of St. Vincent, Nelson, Hornblower, and Mahan, the Navy is wedded to the principle of destroying enemy forces as the basis for conducting other missions, such as the safe delivery of cargoes to foreign ports. But as the British recognized during World War I and World War II, if the enemy fleet stays in or close to port, the cost of going in and destroying it can become unacceptable. The alternative, though less glamorous, is to hem in the enemy by means of a long-range blockade. In the era of the attack submarine, both the offensive strategy and the blockade necessitate the formation of convoys. But the blockade, which can be accompanied by offensive forays, forces the enemy fleet to sally forth from its protective cover, if it wishes to have any impact on the war, and fight at a disadvantage.

This is precisely the problem that the four Soviet fleets can be obliged to face. The fleets in the Baltic and Black seas would have to pass through narrow exits controlled by U.S. allies in order to attack the main lines of communication between the United States and Europe. The other two, the Northern Fleet based near Murmansk and the Pacific Fleet located primarily at Vladivostok and Petropavlovsk, are somewhat less confined. Even so, the Northern Fleet would have to come around the North Cape, run down the Norwegian Sea, and pass through one or more of the channels that separate Greenland, Iceland, and the United Kingdom in order to attack the main Atlantic sea lanes. The Pacific Fleet would face the still more difficult task of escaping from the Sea of Japan and the Sea of Okhotsk through passages controlled for the most part by Japan.

This geography establishes three principal tasks for the navies of the United States and its allies. The first is to construct barriers with mines, submarines, and patrol aircraft at the various chokepoints that will exact a toll from enemy ships and submarines attempting to reach the North Atlantic and Western Pacific. The second is to provide protection for convoys of merchant ships against air attacks and those submarines that get through the barriers. The third is to make sure that Soviet naval forces are not able to evade the barriers for any extended period of time by establishing home ports in such areas as Vietnam, Angola, and Cuba.

This last task could well require the use of carrier battle groups and amphibious forces. It is also plausible that despite efforts to acquire land bases near the oil states of the Persian Gulf, any initial attempt to gain a lodgment for U.S. forces in the area might have to be made by amphibious forces covered by the air power of several carrier battle groups. Whether the carriers would also be needed to protect land operations in Norway or defend convoys in the Atlantic and Pacific is much less clear. In all three instances land bases would be available to provide the necessary air cover.

U.S. allies maintain substantial navies of their own. They can certainly assume responsibility for sealing off the Soviet Baltic and Black Sea fleets and for protecting merchant shipping in the Mediterranean and the Indian Ocean. They can also provide escorts for at least 34 convoys a month in the Atlantic, Mediterranean, and Pacific. With a fleet of 535 ships (counting auxiliaries and underway replenishment ships), which would include 12 carrier battle groups, lift for a full Marine amphibious force, 97 attack submarines, and 80 escorts for convoy duty, the Navy would be able to establish barriers against the Soviet Northern and Pacific Fleets, and escort 8 large convoys a month in the Atlantic and Pacific. It could also project power with carrier battle groups and amphibious forces simultaneously in three contingencies such as might be encountered in the Persian Gulf, Cam Ranh Bay in Vietnam, and Cienfuegos in Cuba.

Despite these impressive capabilities, the administration wants more. Not only is it engaged in the rapid modernization of the existing fleet, but it is also bent on adding three more carrier battle groups, four battleships, fifteen attack submarines, what amounts to another brigade's worth of amphibious lift, and Aegis air defense ships throughout the fleet.

Neither the administration nor the Navy explains in any serious way why these additional forces are needed. Because the Navy does not like to relate its force "requirements" to planning contingencies, one is left to speculate that submariners found 110 attack submarines a convenience in World War II and have stuck with that number ever since, and that because a number of guided missile destroyers will soon have to be replaced, the new ones might as well have the Aegis system on board, even though each one adds $500 million or more to the cost of the ship. Exactly why more amphibious lift is being acquired is even more obscure. The Marine Corps would prefer to have lift available for two amphibious forces, even though it has not made any opposed landing since Inchon in 1950. Perhaps the Corps simply feels that more is better despite the added investment cost of $8 billion and despite the failure to meet the larger "requirement."

The Navy has shown much greater virtuosity in justifying three additional carrier battle groups. The reasons variously advanced have been to maintain a peacetime presence in the Mediterranean, the Western

Pacific, and the Indian Ocean; because national policy requires stationing two carriers in the Mediterranean and three in the Western Pacific, which necessitates a total of fifteen for purposes of rotation; or because an attack on Murmansk or Vladivostok will be needed early in a conflict to obtain command of the seas and to give the president the option of escalating a conventional war "horizontally" in the event of a Soviet attack on an area of vital interest to the United States.

No national policy, however, has required a naval presence in certain oceans or the maintanence of five carriers on overseas stations in peacetime. Rather, the Navy initiated these deployments and then argued for their retention as a way of justifying a particular force structure. As for the offensive against Murmansk or Vladivostok, to the extent that such an attack might have merit, it could be conducted as readily by long-range, land-based aircraft as by carriers, despite the propensity to argue that only naval forces should be allowed to attack naval targets. However, even a brilliantly executed attack on one of the main Soviet naval concentrations would have little assurance of eliminating the attack submarines, the main enemy threat to U.S. and allied sea lines of communication. Furthermore, if the attack depended only on the power of three carrier battle groups, the odds are rather high that all three would be disabled or sunk and that a large part of the Soviet fleet would survive. Indeed, if the Navy is determined to sail into harm's way with surface combatants in the Norwegian and Barents seas, it had better do so with at least nine carrier battle groups. However, this would mean that with a total force of fifteen carriers and a wartime on-station rate of 75 percent, very little in the way of naval air power would be left for other and possibly more important missions. The irresistible conclusion is that either the Navy should forget about Murmansk and Vladivostok as targets for air attack during the early stages of a conventional conflict and settle for twelve carrier battle groups (as it has done before), or it should ask for twenty-four of them. A force of fifteen carrier battle groups seems to be the wrong size, whatever the strategy.

Potential Savings

More military capabilities may seem nice to have, but the programs of the past four years and the plans for the coming five do not mesh very well with identifiable U.S. defense needs of the future. The Reagan administration has certainly done some things that needed doing. It has continued the modernization of weapons and equipment begun in the Ford and Carter administrations. It has increased the supply of spare parts and has built up stocks of modern munitions. It has struggled bravely to reduce the backlog of maintenance and repair, even though the services seem to keep an endless supply of items to add to it. At the same time, however, it has placed more emphasis on the amount by which the defense budget has increased than on what the budget has bought. One consequence is that hard choices have not been made among competing weapons. Another is that mundane but important capabilities have been underfunded or ignored simply because they have lacked the sponsorship of a military service. Overall, the budgets have ballooned more rapidly than warranted by external factors, prudence, or earlier parsimony, and they are now larger than required to cover the deficiencies that can be foreseen.

Nowhere is this more evident than in the funding of the strategic nuclear forces. High accuracy may be desirable for a number of purposes, including the reduction in nuclear yields it permits, and even a capability for the prompt destruction of hard targets may still have a role to play in a second-strike force. But the administration has not adequately explained why it needs the MX, the D-5 (Trident II), which will be much less vulnerable, and the slower but still very accurate cruise missile. Although Soviet active air defenses still remain porous to low-altitude penetrators of the size of the B-52, it is undoubtedly prudent to anticipate the deployment of a look-down, shoot-down capability and to begin deployment of penetrating weapons with smaller radar cross-sections than the current generation of bombers. But it is surely a lack of discipline rather than a demonstration of prudence to proceed simultaneously with the deployment or development of the air-launched cruise missile, the B-1B bomber, an advanced cruise missile, and the stealth bomber. Similarly, it has been agreed for more than a decade that, despite the antiballistic missile treaty and the closing of the one ABM site permitted the United States by the treaty (as amended), a vigorous program of research and development should be pursued on the more traditional methods of intercepting ballistic missiles as well as on lasers and other systems of directed energy mounted on platforms in space. But it is quite another matter to surrender these efforts and their funding to the unbridled optimism of singleminded enthusiasts. Leaving aside the impact of major ABM programs on the strategic competition, it is hard

Table 8. Savings in Nuclear Programs from Reductions in Duplication and Pace, Fiscal Years 1986–89
Billions of dollars

Budget authority	1986	1987	1988	1989	Total
MX missile	3.8	3.1	2.6	0.9	10.4
SICBM	0.5	1.8	1.9	2.4	6.6
B-1B bomber	6.0	0.1	. . .	. . .	6.1
OTH-B radar	0.4	0.3	0.1	. . .	0.8
Stealth bomber	0.5	2.5	2.5	2.5	8.0[a]
Strategic defense initiative	2.4	3.6	4.9	6.0	16.9[b]
Total	13.6	11.4	12.0	11.8	48.8
Outlays	3.5	10.4	12.9	13.8	40.6

Source: *Boston Globe*, February 9, 1985; and author's estimates.
a. The stealth bomber is held in engineering throughout this period; no production is authorized.
b. The strategic defense initiative is frozen at $1.4 billion a year.

to believe that the strategic defense initiative (actually a combination of research ventures already under way) would not benefit from a much less rapid growth in funding than has been projected for it.

A modest reduction in the duplication and excessive pace contained in the administration programs for strategic nuclear modernization and improvement would result in a $49 billion reduction of budget authority and a $41 billion reduction in outlays between fiscal 1986 and 1989 (table 8). Even with these cuts, the United States would be much better able to cover a comprehensive list of targets than is now the case.

The tactical nuclear capabilities are more in need of restructuring than of new weapons, especially weapons that are free as far as the Defense Department is concerned, but that must be funded by the Department of Energy. The conventional forces, on the other hand, are certainly due for a gradual modernization and some expansion, but hardly along the lines being pursued by the administration. For one thing, more funds have been requested than the three services can efficiently obligate in contracts. For another, the pace of acquisition is such that difficult choices will have to be made by future administrations. Either they will have to reduce the defense industrial base because, so much having been done so fast by this administration, there will be a considerable hiatus in the real need to replace the current weapons inventory, or the turnover of that inventory will have to begin before the useful lives of the weapons (averaging about twenty years) have ended. Finally, it should be evident that the allocation of resources has been determined more by service traditions and the inclination of each to prepare for its own preferred war than by integrated national security needs. The Army has designed its new M-1 tank independently of the intercontinental airlift available to move it and struggles to obtain close air support for its divisions by building fragile attack helicopters that are more costly than the sturdier fixed-wing aircraft for which the Air Force has the primary responsibility. Although close-air-support aircraft deliver enormous firepower and are the acme of maneuver warfare, the Air Force concentrates most of its tactical resources on preparations to wage a campaign of deep air superiority and interdiction that by most accounts will have a major impact on the land campaign only after the decisive ground battles have been fought—battles on which close-air-support aircraft could have an immediate and direct effect. The Marine Corps, doubtful that the Navy will provide its amphibious operations with carrier-based air cover or that carrier air wings will ever be designed or trained to give them the close air support needed for a forced landing against a well-prepared enemy, has looked for its salvation to the return of the battleship with its big guns and to the acquisition of the inefficient AV-8B aircraft, which can at least take off and land on some of the larger amphibious ships and thus substitute for carrier-based aircraft. Meanwhile, the Navy, like George Leigh Mallory, climbs its Everest of the 600-ship fleet because it is there.

Free enterprise has its place, but its place is not in the Pentagon. Regulation of uncontrolled service entrepreneurship not only would permit major savings of budget authority and outlays, but it would also allow the funding of larger ground and close-air-support forces, both of which are needed far more than additional long-legged fighter-attack aircraft and their carrier-based equivalents.

Additional savings can be made by substituting fast sealift for further airlift and by introducing new criteria to determine the need for modern munitions. The Air Force claims that a national objective requires it to seek an intercontinental airlift capacity of 66 million ton/miles a day. This compares with the 32.4 million ton/miles a day it can currently lift, primarily with 70 C-5A and 234 C-141 aircraft. However, even a doubled capability—much of it to be provided by the hybrid C-17—would allow delivery of fewer than 15,000 tons a day to central Europe and around 7,000 tons a day to the head of the Persian Gulf, substantially less than would be needed by the three services in either theater during the deployment times supposedly available.

There is another paradox here. The national "requirement" arises from those contingencies that postulate superhuman efforts on the part of the Soviet Union and its satellites and sluggish reactions on the part of the United States. However, if it is assumed that U.S. leaders will always procrastinate during a crisis, 66 million ton/miles a day understates the amount of intercontinental airlift that should be acquired, especially in the event of two or more simultaneous contingencies. On the other hand, if more realistic contingencies are assumed and U.S. leaders react promptly, current airlift combined with a buildup of fast sealift—much cheaper to acquire and operate—would be able to satisfy expected needs. In the circumstances, it makes sense to review these choices and examine the assumptions on which they are based rather than to plunge into the costly expansion of airlift advocated by the Air Force.

As for modern munitions, when they can cost anywhere from several thousand to several million dollars a round (as in the case of the Phoenix missile for the Navy's F-14 fighter), it is essential to determine with some precision how many of them might be needed in a major conflict. At present, some of the requirements for war reserve stocks are based on the number of targets that might be encountered in one or more theaters. More often, however, the "requirement" rests on daily consumption rates extrapolated to as many as 180 days. What is more, these daily rates have undergone a substantial inflation based on the last Arab-Israeli war when there were seven days of intense firing—which may or may not be representative of a more extended campaign in which consumption has become more disciplined. It is hardly surprising that, faced with this almost open-ended requirement, the administration should have put so much money into war reserve stocks, have made so little apparent progress in their buildup, and have received so much criticism for underfunding combat readiness.

While much of this criticism has been unwarranted, it is unfortunate that the Pentagon has not responded to it more effectively. Rather than accept the war reserve objectives of the military services as sensible, senior defense officials need to take two steps. First, they should review the assumption that Soviet and satellite forces have accumulated war reserve stocks for a worldwide campaign of long duration. Such an assumption is hardly consistent with the emphasis of Soviet military leaders on fighting short, blitzkrieg-style wars, and their relatively recent conversion to the possibility that a conventional conflict will not quickly escalate to a nuclear exchange. Furthermore, their military budget, large though it may be, does not appear to be nearly large enough to allow the rapid accumulation of the enormous war reserve stocks that would be required to operate the 194 divisions, more than 5,000 tactical fighters, and 1,000 ships that, according to the Pentagon, constitute the current Soviet order of battle. Even if the actual order of battle is much more modest, as is probably the case, the USSR, like the United States, almost certainly has difficulty at current budgetary levels in stocking modern munitions for more than a month of intense conflict.

As a second step, officials need to consider whether modern munitions will prove as lethal as they are supposed to be. If they are, the armed forces will probably have run out of targets well before 180 days of combat have elapsed. If they are not, if they are only a modest improvement over "dumb" munitions, the question arises as to why, at such great cost, the services want to substitute them for the much cheaper bullets, shells, and bombs with which they are already well supplied.

The truth about the lethality of these weapons will probably come to lie somewhere in between. Should that be the case, considering the large investment already made in the current generation of "smart" munitions, a strong case can be made for slowing down rather than accelerating further purchases and waiting until consumption rates are related to targets before deciding on the objectives for the war reserve stocks.

Table 9 illustrates how increases and decreases could be made in programs for the ground, tactical air, naval, and rapid deployment forces in order to ensure that future capabilities are more suited to potential threats. Table 10 measures the effects of making selected decreases in nuclear and conventional programs retroactive to fiscal 1983 in the form of congressional rescissions. Table 11 estimates the impact of holding future procurement of modern munitions at fiscal 1985 levels. As is evident, large savings can still be made in defense budget authority and outlays for the conventional forces without any reduction in the ability of the United States to fulfill its international obligations. Together with the savings possible in the programs for the nuclear forces, they would permit a major contribution to the reduction of the federal deficit without reducing the effectiveness of the U.S. defense establishment (table 12).

Congressional Action

Realistically, however, Congress has proved unable or unwilling to cancel major programs without the initiative of the executive branch.

The Reagan administration has touted the reductions it has made in previous defense budgets before they were even submitted to Congress, but the services have given up none of their more cherished aspirations in this process of alleged economizing. For its part, Congress has been remarkably receptive to the administration's main requests. It began the decade by adding to the original requests, and only since 1983 has it throttled back on the rate of real growth in defense budget authority and outlays (table 13). Despite this swing toward modest restraint, no major weapon system has been canceled. Indeed, the real growth in investment, especially when compared with that of the operating and support accounts (table 14), has been impressive. Not surprisingly, even the MX missile survives, however precariously, despite having become the annual symbol of opposition to the nuclear buildup.

This is not to say that Congress has refused to cut the investment accounts. In fiscal 1985 alone, it reduced the administration's original request by $20 billion, of which $10 billion came out of the procurement account. Admittedly, some of these reductions were belatedly volunteered by the three services but only as a result of pressure on the president and congressional determination to make cuts. What the reductions indicate, however, is that without leadership and cooperation from the executive branch, and the Defense Department in particular, Congress finds it virtually impossible to do more than whittle away at line items in the defense budget and to stretch out programs rather than cancel them. Unless or until economic problems worsen as a consequence of the federal deficit, that whittling may be all that can be anticipated from the coming budget debates. The White House, for its part, has rejected the proposals from the Office of Management and Budget to wring $58 billion or more out of defense spending during the next three fiscal years. It apparently intends to protect as much of its huge investment program as possible, offer a pretense of reductions, and accept defense cuts only under extreme pressure from Congress.

Budget Strategies

It must remain uncertain whether defense can be expected to make significant contributions to reductions in the federal deficit under these conditions. In principle, large savings are still possible because so much fat has been incorporated into the administration's programs. In practice it will not prove easy to produce major reductions, forgo the cancellation

Table 9. Decreases and Increases in Non-Nuclear Programs, Fiscal Years 1986–89
Billions of dollars

Program	Action	1986	1987	1988	1989	Total
Decreases in budget authority						
Army						
M-1 tank	reduce to 600	0.3	0.3	0.3	0.3	1.2
M-2 fighting vehicle	reduce to 600	0.4	0.4	0.4	0.4	1.6
Binary chemical munitions	cancel	0.4	0.7	1.3	3.0	5.4
Division air defense gun	cancel	0.7	0.4	0.1	0.1	1.3
Patriot air defense missile	cancel procurement	1.4	1.2	0.9	0.6	4.1
Total Army decreases		3.2	3.0	3.0	4.4	13.6
Navy						
AV-8B fighter	cut production in half	0.5	0.4	0.5	0.5	1.9
P-3C patrol aircraft	reduce from 9 to 6 a year	0.2	0.2	0.2	0.2	0.8
E-2 early warning	reduce from 6 to 3 a year	0.2	0.2	0.2	0.2	0.8
JVX vertical lift	cancel procurement	...	...	0.1	1.3	1.4
EA-6B aircraft	reduce from 6 to 3 a year	0.2	0.2	0.1	0.2	0.7
F-14A/D fighter	cut production in half	0.6	0.5	0.6	0.8	2.5
F/A-18 aircraft	reduce to 60 a year	1.2	1.3	1.4	1.2	5.1
Battleship reactivation	cancel	...	0.5	...	...	0.5
SSN-688 attack submarine	reduce from 4 to 2 a year	1.2	1.2	1.3	1.4	5.1
DDG-51 Aegis destroyer	reduce from 5 to 3 a year	...	...	1.8	1.9	3.7
CG-47 Aegis cruiser	cancel	3.3	3.5	2.6	2.8	12.2
LSD-41 landing ship dock	cancel	0.5	0.5	...	...	1.0
LHD-1 amphibious assault ship	cancel	1.4	0.1	1.5	1.6	4.6
Total Navy decreases		9.3	8.6	10.3	12.1	40.3

Air Force						
F-15 fighter	reduce production to 36 a year	0.3	0.5	1.4	1.0	3.2
F-16 fighter	reduce production to 120 a year	1.9	1.7	1.7	1.8	7.1
LANTIRN navigation system	cancel	0.5	0.8	0.7	0.6	2.6
C-5B airlift aircraft	cancel	2.6	2.3	. .	. .	4.9
C-17 airlift aircraft	cancel	0.4	0.6	2.6	2.7	6.3
Total Air Force decreases		5.7	5.9	6.4	6.1	24.1
Total decreases in budget authority		18.2	17.5	19.7	22.6	78.0
Increases in budget authority						
Army National Guard and reserve		2.7	2.8	3.0	3.3	11.8
Air Force National Guard and reserve		2.5	2.7	3.0	3.1	11.3
Navy sealift (25 ships)		1.2	1.2	1.3	1.3	5.0
Total increases in budget authority		6.4	6.7	7.3	7.7	28.1
Effects on outlays						
Decreases in budget authority		2.6	9.0	14.0	17.0	42.6
Increases in budget authority		0.9	3.2	5.1	6.2	15.4
Total savings on outlays		1.7	5.8	8.9	10.8	27.2

Source: Author's estimates.

Table 10. Estimated Decreases in Defense Budget Authority Resulting from Potential Congressional Rescissions, Fiscal Years 1983–85
Billions of dollars

Program	Action	1983	1984	1985	Total
Nuclear systems					
MX missile	cancel	1.2	2.1	2.5	5.8
B-1B bomber	cancel	2.0	2.4	4.1	8.5
SICBM	cancel	..	0.2	0.2	0.4
Strategic defense initiative	cut in half	..	0.4	0.5	0.9
OTH-B radar	cancel	..	..	0.3	0.3
Total		3.2	5.1	7.6	15.9
Non-nuclear systems					
M-1 tank	reduce from 720 to 600	0.3	0.3	0.3	0.9
Division air defense gun (DIVAD)	cancel	0.5	0.6	0.6	1.7
Patriot air defense missile	cancel	0.8	1.0	1.3	3.1
AV-8B fighter	cancel	0.2	0.2	1.0	1.4
F-14 fighter	cut production in half	0.4	0.4	0.6	1.4
Aircraft carrier (CVN)	cancel 2	5.0	..	..	5.0
Landing ship dock (LSD-41)	cancel 3	0.4	0.4	0.5	1.3
Amphibious assault ship (LHD-1)	cancel 1	0.1	1.4	..	1.5
F-15 fighter	cut production in half	0.7	0.7	1.0	2.4
C-5B airlift aircraft	cancel	0.4	0.7	1.0	2.1
C-17 airlift aircraft	cancel	..	..	0.1	0.1
Total		8.8	5.7	6.4	20.9
Total decreases in budget authority[a]		12.0	10.8	14.0	36.8

Sources: *Department of Defense Annual Report, Fiscal Year 1984; Fiscal Year 1985*; and author's estimates.
a. Resulting reductions in outlays would be $9.2 billion in fiscal 1986, $5.7 billion in 1987, $2.6 billion in 1988, and $1.3 billion in 1989, for a total of $18.8 billion.

Table 11. Estimated Savings from a Freeze on the Acquisition of Modern Munitions, Fiscal Years 1986–89
Billions of dollars

Service	1986	1987	1988	1989	Total
Army	0.5	. . .	. . .	. . .	0.5
Navy/Marine Corps	0.6	0.9	1.5	1.0	4.0
Air Force	0.8	1.2	1.5	1.6	5.1
Savings in budget authority	1.9	2.1	3.0	2.6	9.6
Savings in outlays	0.4	1.3	2.1	2.7	6.5

Source: Author's estimates.

Table 12. Potential Decreases and Increases in Nuclear and Non-Nuclear Programs, Fiscal Years 1986–89
Billions of dollars

Authority and outlays	1986	1987	1988	1989	Total
Budget authority					
Nuclear programs	13.6	11.4	12.0	11.8	48.8
Non-nuclear programs	18.2	17.5	19.7	22.6	78.0
Modern munitions	1.9	2.1	3.0	2.6	9.6
Rescissions	. . .	. . .	. . .	. . .	. . .
Decreases in budget authority	33.7	31.0	34.7	37.0	136.4
Increases in budget authority	6.4	6.7	7.3	7.7	28.1
Net decreases	27.3	24.3	27.4	29.3	108.3
Outlays					
Nuclear programs	3.5	10.4	12.9	13.8	40.6
Non-nuclear programs	2.6	9.0	14.0	17.0	42.6
Modern munitions	0.4	1.3	2.1	2.7	6.5
Rescissions	9.2	5.7	2.6	1.3	18.8
Decreases in outlays	15.7	26.4	31.6	34.8	108.5
Increases in outlays	0.9	3.2	5.1	6.2	15.4
Net decreases	14.8	23.2	26.5	28.6	93.1

Sources: Tables 8, 9, 10, and 11; and author's estimates.

Table 13. Congressional Action on the Defense Budget, Fiscal Years 1980–85
Billions of dollars of obligational authority

Action	1980	1981	1982	1983	1984	1985
Presidential request	135.5	158.7	226.5[a]	258.0	274.1	305.7
Congressional appropriation	141.5	177.0	212.4	239.3	258.2	285.3
Difference	+6.0	+18.3	−14.1	−18.7	−15.9	−20.4
Appropriations as percent of request	1.044	1.115	0.938	0.928	0.942	0.933

Sources: Alice Maroni, *Analysis of Congressional Changes to the FY 1984 Defense Budget*, Congressional Research Service, Library of Congress, Report no. 84-763F (October 2, 1984), p. 7; *Department of Defense Annual Report, Fiscal Year 1980, Fiscal Year 1981, Fiscal Year 1982, Fiscal Year 1983, Fiscal Year 1984,* and *Fiscal Year 1985;* and author's estimates.

a. The original submission by President Carter amounted to $196.4 billion; President Reagan subsequently submitted supplemental requests to increase both the 1981 and 1982 appropriations.

Table 14. Growth in Defense Investment and Operating Accounts, Fiscal Years 1980–85
Billions of dollars of budget authority unless otherwise noted

Accounts	1980	1981	1982	1983	1984	1985
Investment						
Procurement	35.3	54.8	64.5	80.4	86.0	96.8
Research, development, test,						
and evaluation	13.6	18.9	20.1	22.8	26.9	31.5
Military construction	2.3	3.8	4.9	4.5	4.5	5.5
Total	51.2	77.5	89.5	107.7	117.4	133.8
Constant 1985 dollars	69.0	93.9	101.4	117.1	122.7	133.8
Operating						
Military personnel	31.0	36.7	42.9	45.7	48.6	51.9
Operation and maintenance	46.4	55.2	62.5	66.5	70.9	78.2
Family housing	1.5	2.0	2.2	2.7	2.7	2.9
Management funds	1.3	0.5	2.5	1.1	2.5	1.6
Total	80.2	94.4	110.1	116.0	124.7	134.6
Constant 1985 dollars	108.1	114.4	124.7	126.1	130.3	134.6
Real growth (percent)						
Investment						
Year-to-year	...	36.1	8.0	15.5	4.8	9.0
Cumulative	...	36.1	47.0	69.7	77.8	93.9
Operating						
Year-to-year	...	5.8	9.0	1.1	3.3	3.3
Cumulative	...	5.8	15.4	16.7	20.5	24.5

Sources: *Department of Defense Annual Report, Fiscal Year 1980, Fiscal Year 1981, Fiscal Year 1982, Fiscal Year 1983, Fiscal Year 1984, Fiscal Year 1985, and Fiscal Year 1986.*

of the more redundant and marginal weapons (some of which are now protected by multiyear procurement contracts), and maintain a balanced military establishment. In such an establishment, military and civilian pay would be increased by the expected rate of inflation; the combat effectiveness, strategic mobility, and sustainability of existing forces would be maintained; and modernization of the weapons inventory would still proceed, but at a much slower pace.

To test the possibilities of balance and cuts but few cancellations, three illustrative budget plans are presented, each covering fiscal years 1986, 1987, and 1988. Each is compared with the administration's budget plan for these same three years (table 15). In the first, budget authority is allowed to increase in real terms by 3 percent a year from the 1985 base of $284.7 billion. In the second the real increase is held to one percent. In the third a freeze is imposed, although increases to compensate for inflation are allowed.

Table 15. Reagan Administration's Defense Budget Plan and Three Alternatives, Fiscal Years 1986–89
Billions of dollars unless otherwise specified

	Fiscal years			
Item	*1985*	*1986*	*1987*	*1988*
Budget authority				
Administration plan	284.7	313.7	354.0	401.6
3 percent solution	284.7	304.5	328.0	352.7
1 percent solution	284.7	298.6	315.4	332.6
Freeze	284.7	295.6	309.2	322.8
Outlays				
Administration plan	246.3	277.5	312.3	348.6
3 percent solution	246.3	272.4	296.1	319.9
1 percent solution	246.3	269.2	287.9	305.6
Freeze	246.3	267.6	283.8	298.4
Rate of inflation				
Budget authority				
Year-to-year	. . .	1.040	1.043	1.042
Cumulative	. . .	1.040	1.085	1.130
Outlays				
Year-to-year	. . .	1.038	1.045	1.045
Cumulative	. . .	1.038	1.085	1.134

Source: *Department of Defense Annual Report, Fiscal Year 1986*, p. 78; *Budget of the United States Government, Fiscal Year 1986*, pp. 9–59; and author's estimates.

Exactly how these hypothetical controls on budget authority would affect defense outlays depends on two factors: the degree to which expenditures would result from budget authority obligated but not spent in prior years and the distribution of the new budget authority among the major appropriation accounts. Beginning in fiscal 1986 (October 1, 1985) the backlog of defense budget authority will amount to around $243 billion. Of that total, about $106 billion will be spent in 1986 unless Congress dictates major rescissions in the budget authority for prior years. Outlays thereafter will be determined to a large extent by the size and composition of the authority added to the backlog in fiscal 1986 and 1987. If the budgets for those two years and for 1988 are heavily weighted toward procurement, as they have been during the last four years, the backlog will continue to grow rapidly, a stream of essentially uncontrollable outlays will constitute a major component of future defense spending, and first-year outlays from new budget authority will be relatively low. If, on the other hand, procurement (and to a lesser extent research, development, test, and evaluation and military construction) are stretched out substantially, the percentage of new budget authority spent in the first year will be relatively high, and future-year outlays will grow less rapidly.

Because defense spending has these characteristics—with what are known as fast and slow money—any strategy for reducing the defense budget will be affected by both the magnitude of the savings that are desired and by when they are wanted. If large savings are sought, and needed in the next three years, it will be difficult not to cut the fast-money accounts, which consist of military and civilian pay, operation and maintenance, family housing for the military, and the large management funds. However, if the demand for defense savings in the first and second years is relatively modest, and the objective is as much to develop a sustainable budget course as to produce short-term savings, cuts in budget authority should concentrate more heavily on the slow-money accounts, that is, procurement, research, development, test, and evaluation and military construction.

What would have to be done to the defense program in order to live within the overall constraints that have been hypothesized? According to the secretary of defense, these conditions could be met only by a wholesale slaughter of vital weapons and equipment and would therefore be unacceptable. As a substitute he offers a five-year defense plan that averages 6.6 percent a year real growth and produces savings in outlays of $27.7 billion during the next three fiscal years. The appropriations requested by the secretary for 1986 and proposed for 1987 and 1988 are listed in table 16.

One of the more significant savings in outlays assumed by the secretary comes from a reduction of 5 percent in pay for civilian personnel in 1986. This cut, which would affect more than a million defense employees, would also reduce budget authority and outlays in subsequent fiscal years because future pay increases would be computed from this lower base. There is also a reduction in the request for military pay. Part of it is achieved by transforming the bulk of the originally planned increase to 1985, thereby increasing the deficit for that year, and proposing a smaller increase in 1986. Another part comes from withholding the cost of living adjustment for retired military personnel and reducing the estimate of retired pay accrual that will have to be deposited in the trust fund now established for them. Both cuts will result in savings during subsequent fiscal years.

Table 16. President Reagan's Defense Program, Fiscal Years 1985–88
Billions of dollars

Appropriation title	1985	1986	1987	1988
Military personnel	68.9	73.4	79.6	85.5
Operation and maintenance	78.2	82.5	95.0	108.9
Procurement	96.8	106.8	122.4	141.2
Research, development, test, and evaluation	31.5	39.3	42.6	49.3
Military construction	5.5	7.1	8.9	10.5
Family housing and homeowners' assistance program	2.9	3.3	3.9	4.3
Revolving and management funds	1.6	1.9	2.4	2.8
Trust funds, receipts, and deductions	−0.6	−0.7	−0.8	−0.8
Proposed legislation	...	0.2	...	0.1
Budget authority (051 account)[a]	284.7	313.7	354.0	401.6
Defense-related functions	7.8	8.5	9.3	9.9
Budget authority (050 account)[b]	292.5	322.2	363.3	411.5
Outlays (051 account)	246.3	277.5	312.3	348.6
Outlays (050 account)	253.8	285.7	321.2	358.4

Source: *Budget of the United States Government, Fiscal Year 1986*, p. 5-5.

a. The 051 account represents Defense Department military functions; defense civil functions (cemeteries and Corps of Engineers among others) are carried in a separate account. Because of rounding, individual titles may not add to totals shown.

b. The 050 account (national defense) contains atomic energy defense activities, the civil defense functions of the Federal Emergency Management Agency, and other defense-related activities as well as defense military functions.

Other savings are achieved because inflation rates lower than were assumed in earlier estimates are applied to the purchase of goods and services and because the price of fuel consumed by defense is expected to decline still further. Overall, however, reductions in outlays will be modest during the coming three years, and both budget authority and outlays will continue to grow more rapidly than either the federal budget or the GNP.

Secretary Weinberger has computed the savings he expects to realize by comparing his budget with the amount proposed in the so-called Rose Garden compromise of August 1984. Greater illumination comes from comparing the budgets for 1986–89 that the secretary submitted on February 1, 1984, with the budgets for the same years that he proposed on February 4, 1985 (table 17). The gap in budget authority between the two is $36 billion in fiscal 1986, but it shrinks to $7.3 billion by 1989 and would completely disappear if last year's estimate were repriced using current deflators. In other words, after what seems to be a one-year

Table 17. Original and Revised Defense Budgets, Fiscal Years 1986–89
Billions of dollars

Authority and outlays	1986	1987	1988	1989
Budget authority				
As of February 1, 1984	349.6	379.2	411.5	446.1
As of February 4, 1985	313.7	354.0	401.6	438.8
Difference	35.9	25.2	9.9	7.3
Outlays				
As of February 1, 1984	301.8	339.2	369.8	398.8
As of February 4, 1985	277.5	312.3	348.6	382.3
Difference	24.3	26.9	21.2	16.5

Sources: *Department of Defense Annual Report, Fiscal Year 1985*, p. 71; *Fiscal Year 1986*, p. 78.

detour from his chosen path, Mr. Weinberger gets back on his original track with remarkable celerity.

It is by no means clear that the secretary has suffered much of a setback from even this large reduction in 1986. Table 18 compares the appropriations estimated a year ago with those now being requested. All the accounts suffer losses between 1984 and 1985 with the single exception of research, development, test, and evaluation, which increases by $1.5 billion even though the current request for the strategic defense initiative is virtually identical with the proposal of a year ago. The two big losers, at least on the surface, are operation and maintenance and procurement. Even here, however, the loss is probably less than meets the eye. More modest inflation than was expected as of 1984 probably accounts for at least $2 billion of the reduction. Some of the decline also comes from the pay cut handed to civilian workers of the department and from lower fuel prices. Flying, steaming, and driving hours—already at high levels in 1985—may not have been increased as rapidly as earlier planned. The secretary may even have frozen other accounts in the belated realization that no matter how much he strives to abolish the backlog of maintenance and repair, the list of "required" projects keeps growing longer and more expensive.

How as much as $19 billion could be made to vanish from procurement proves more difficult to understand. Although production rates in some instances are now lower than were planned a year ago, the secretary has given up very little in the way of major programs, significant duplication, or the rapid pace at which everything is being funded. The principal strategic nuclear systems are to get the same amount of money that was projected for them a year ago. Although four fewer new ships are

Table 18. Original and Revised Defense Appropriation Requests, Fiscal Year 1986
Billions of dollars

Appropriation	Original (2/1/84)	Revised (2/4/85)[a]	Difference[a]
Military personnel	77.0	73.4	−3.6
Operation and maintenance	92.9	82.5	−10.4
Procurement	126.0	106.8	−19.2
Research, development, test, and evaluation	37.8	39.3	+1.5
Military construction	10.0	7.1	−2.9
Family housing and homeowners' assistance program	3.8	3.3	−0.5
Revolving and management funds	3.1	1.9	−1.2
Trust funds, receipts, and deductions	−0.9	−0.7	+0.2
Proposed legislation	. . .	0.2	+0.2
Budget authority	349.7	313.7	−36.0

Sources: *Budget of the United States Government, Fiscal Year 1985*, p. 5-10; *Department of Defense Annual Report, Fiscal Year 1986*, p. 293.
a. Items may not add because of rounding.

requested than in the earlier plan, an additional three older ships would undergo modernization, and the production rate of the M-1 tank is actually scheduled to be higher. Only tactical aircraft seem to fare more poorly, in part no doubt because unit costs have increased.

In the circumstances the suspicion is bound to arise that even if the secretary still had the $19 billion, he would not quite know what to do with it. Such suspicion may be unjustified, but it is noteworthy that current budget authority is being spent more slowly with each passing year, particularly where the investment accounts are concerned. What is more, the backlog of budget authority is growing more rapidly than was projected only a year ago, even though the funding available for 1985 is $20 billion less than was assumed when the previous estimate was made. Inputs continue to grow, but outputs do not appear to rise commensurately. Eventually, though, all the bills will come due, outlays will finally reflect these large and expanding commitments, and a future president will have to decide whether to begin a new round of still more costly modernization or allow the defense industrial base to languish while the current round is absorbed.

That is one way to go. However, it is perfectly possible and quite acceptable from the standpoint of defense planning to live within any

Table 19. Appropriation Accounts for Alternative Defense Budgets, Fiscal Years 1986–88
Billions of dollars

Appropriation title	3 percent solution			1 percent solution			Freeze		
	1986	1987	1988	1986	1987	1988	1986	1987	1988
Military personnel	71.2	75.1	79.0	71.2	75.1	79.0	71.2	75.1	79.0
Operation and maintenance	83.1	88.6	94.3	81.9	86.1	90.3	81.3	84.8	88.3
Procurement	107.7	120.0	133.2	103.1	109.9	117.2	100.7	105.0	109.4
Research, development, test, and evaluation	32.8	34.2	35.6	32.8	34.2	35.6	32.8	34.2	35.6
Military construction	5.7	6.0	6.2	5.7	6.0	6.2	5.7	6.0	6.2
Family housing and homeowners' assistance	3.0	3.1	3.3	3.0	3.1	3.3	3.0	3.1	3.3
Revolving and management funds	1.0	1.0	1.1	0.9	1.0	1.0	0.9	1.0	1.0
Budget authority	304.5	328.0	352.7	298.6	315.4	332.6	295.6	309.2	322.8
Outlays									
Administration baseline[a]	286.2	321.5	358.8	286.2	321.5	358.8	286.2	321.5	358.8
Alternatives	272.4	296.1	319.9	269.2	287.9	305.6	267.6	283.8	298.4
Difference	13.8	25.4	38.9	17.0	33.6	53.2	18.6	37.7	60.4
Cumulative difference	13.8	39.2	78.1	17.0	50.6	103.8	18.6	56.3	116.7

Source: Author's estimates.
a. The administration baseline outlays are the numbers accepted by President Reagan as part of the "Rose Garden" compromise of August 1984. The savings in defense outlays claimed by the administration in fiscal 1986 ($8.7 billion), 1987 ($9.0 billion), and 1988 ($10.0 billion) are measured from the baseline or "Rose Garden" numbers, as are the savings estimated for the three alternatives.

one of the proposed budgetary constraints simply by taking the following steps:

—Allow military and civilian pay to increase by the estimated rate of inflation.

—Freeze in real terms the appropriation accounts for research, development, test, and evaluation, military construction, and military family housing.

—Freeze selected items in the operation and maintenance account (flying hours, ship and land operations, equipment modernization, and real property maintenance activities) in real terms because they are already being funded at high levels.

—Cut the procurement account by whatever amount is needed to bring total budget authority in line with the aggregate amount required by the specified rate of real growth.

Table 19 shows what the appropriation accounts would look like for 0, 1, and 3 percent rates of real growth. It also estimates the outlays that would result from prior year obligations and this particular mix of cuts in the appropriation accounts.

Obviously, the reductions about which there would be the greatest outcry are those that would address procurement and research, development, test, and evaluation. These reductions would, however, be much less damaging to the overall health of the defense establishment than they sound. They would, after all, occur in the wake of unprecedented peacetime real growth in these accounts during the past four years. In the case of procurement, even the most severe reductions (those required by the freeze budget) can be accommodated by canceling the MX missile and a small number of other programs, stretching out other major procurement, making some rescissions, and continuing the acquisition of modern munitions at 1985 levels of effort (table 20). Much of the reduction in research, development, test, and evaluation can come from ending the growth in funding the strategic defense initiative and from stretching out the development of the stealth bomber.

Some will no doubt contend that stretching out procurement will prove particularly damaging. Not only is it supposed to harm the essential and finely calibrated buildup launched in 1981 and drive up costs, but it will allegedly send a wrong signal to the Soviet leadership and undermine the administration's efforts to negotiate a reduction of nuclear arms. However, it is at least as plausible that the pace of the buildup has been excessive in light of the threat and the need and that it should be slowed

Table 20. Examples of Reductions in Procurement Required by Alternative Budgets, Fiscal Years 1986–88
Outlays in billions of dollars

Programs	3 percent solution			1 percent solution			Freeze		
	1986	1987	1988	1986	1987	1988	1986	1987	1988
Total reduction required	2.4	8.2	11.4	3.1	11.4	18.7	3.4	13.0	22.4
Nuclear programs									
MX missile	0.7	2.5	3.0	0.7	2.5	3.0	0.7	2.5	3.0
OTH-B radar	0.1	0.1	0.2	0.1	0.1	0.2	0.1	0.1	0.2
B-1 bomber	...	...	...	...	...	...	0.6	2.7	2.2
Stealth bomber	...	0.3	1.4	...	0.3	1.4	...	0.3	1.4
Non-nuclear programs									
DIVAD	0.6	0.6	0.5	0.6	0.6	0.5	0.6	0.6	0.5
Patriot missile	...	...	...	0.2	0.8	1.2	0.1	0.8	1.2
Binary chemicals	...	...	...	...	0.3	0.7	...	0.3	0.7
Modern munitions	...	...	2.1	0.4	1.3	2.1	0.4	1.3	2.1
Navy ships[a]	0.2	0.8	2.1	0.2	0.8	2.1	0.2	0.8	2.1
Rescission of prior-year ships[b]	...	...	...	...	...	...	1.4	1.4	1.4
Navy aircraft[a]	0.4	1.5	2.6	0.4	1.5	2.6	0.4	1.5	2.6
Air Force aircraft[a]	0.6	3.1	5.2	0.6	3.1	5.2	0.6	3.1	5.2
Total	2.6	8.9	15.0	3.2	11.3	19.0	5.1	15.4	22.6

Sources: Tables 8, 9, 10, 11, 16; and author's estimates.
a. For detail, see table 9.
b. For detail, see table 10.

independently of fiscal considerations. Furthermore, the increased unit costs that could result from stretching out procurement are likely to be more than counterbalanced by a quicker solution of the economic problems caused by large federal deficits and by future savings in modernization programs as the useful lives of major weapons are extended to the appropriate average age of twenty years. Finally, Soviet leaders will probably be less impressed than the president and the secretary of defense by the notion that increased defense spending automatically leads to increased political and military capability. In their own experience, larger budgets have not seemed to improve their lot or their bargaining position.

Institutional Change

Regrettably, it remains doubtful whether the United States will fare any better despite the resources being lavished on defense. Too many programs are being funded too rapidly. Duplication is excessive, and the misallocation of funds is such that carrier battle groups and penetrating bombers receive the lion's share of the appropriations, while the more essential ground forces, close-air-support aircraft, and fast sealift do substantially less well.

In the short run it may be necessary to accept these commitments while minimizing their costs. But several actions will surely have to be taken in the longer run to ensure a more sensible and orderly evolution of the defense establishment. At the root of the current failure is a decisionmaking system that has become a parody of modern defense management. The original system, mostly instituted in the early 1960s, resulted from President Eisenhower's recognition that neither the military services nor the Joint Chiefs of Staff would be able or even willing to resolve their endless disputes about budgets, objectives, and forces; that unification of the services would solve nothing because the advocates of air power, submarine warfare, tanks, and missiles would continue their advocacy even though dressed in uniforms of the same color (usually and derisively considered to be purple); and that only a secretary of defense with the power to take initiatives and resolve disputes could hope to bring the combatants under control. This recognition led to successive revisions of the National Security Act of 1947. Those revisions in turn permitted first Thomas Gates and then Robert McNamara, strongly supported by their respective presidents, to become the true leaders of the Pentagon.

Inevitably, such an exercise of power led to bitterness on the part of the services. Upon becoming secretary of defense in 1969, Melvin Laird attempted to dispel this hostility by endorsing the concept of participatory management. After only a year of decontrol, however, he began to reverse the process. Until 1981 the trend toward more centralized planning resumed, though unevenly. But since the advent of the Reagan administration not only has decontrol come back into vogue, there has also been a full-scale retreat to the feudal reign of the 1950s that President Eisenhower worked so hard to end.

The planning, programming, and budgeting system still exists, but the services dominate the process and no one seriously challenges their priorities. A small number of programs—the MX, the B-1B, and the 600-ship navy—are artifacts of the 1980 presidential campaign and Mr. Reagan's criticism of the Carter administration. Along with the strategic defense initiative, they are protected from service skepticism, bickering, and cuts. But the bulk of what is being funded, including redundant weapons, reflects long-standing military wishes and a long-standing military propensity to disregard costs and marginal utility in expressing those wishes. Objectives are set, "requirements" established, and the bill presented. The secretary of defense and his deputy preside over the process and, like the good fairies, set a limit on the number of wishes that will be granted in a given year. But it is rare that they lead and even rarer that they choose. With so much budget authority to disburse and so little sensitivity to opportunity costs, choice may not even seem necessary. The upshot is that unless discipline is restored to the decisionmaking process—and it is already late in the day for that—one of two eventualities can be anticipated. Either the rapid accumulation of weapons will continue, creating a growing demand for their maintenance, modernization, and replacement, with defense claiming a rising share of the federal budget and the gross national product. Or a famine will replace the current feast, and the military establishment will inherit a vast array of new vehicles, ships, aircraft, and missiles that it cannot afford to operate and maintain.

Rules of the Game

Neither eventuality is to be desired. Although the outside world may not be quite as dangerous a place in which to venture as the administration has suggested, neither is it a place in which to venture unarmed. What the country needs after the enormous surge of the last four years is a defense capability that evolves gradually and steadily in response to a realistic estimate of what the Soviet Union can and will do and what modern technology can reliably provide. To meet that need, a number of steps are essential.

First, the secretary of defense, instead of becoming Mr. Outside—the representative and advocate of the department—must once again use his great legal powers to restore discipline to the planning, programming, and budgeting system and make the choices that the services and the Joint Chiefs have repeatedly demonstrated they are unable or unwilling to make.

Second, the secretary must lay out and stick to a modernization strategy that avoids the pell-mell acquisition of weapons (which only leads to systems that do not work properly and to future block obsolescence) and spreads out the replacement process over a period of twenty years.

Third, the degree of combat effectiveness (usually referred to as readiness and sustainability) that should be maintained by existing forces, including reserve forces, must be explicitly determined rather than left to service tradition and the availability of funds after investment wishes have been satisfied.

Fourth, the type and amount of intercontinental mobility must be related to the size and composition of the armed forces and their ability realistically to use it. There is no sense in maintaining costly active-duty units that cannot be deployed to threatened theaters in a timely enough fashion to deter or halt an opposing threat.

Finally, the secretary would do well to close his ears to the siren songs of those who advocate such nostrums as a maritime strategy, horizontal escalation, and war-winning nuclear abstractions. The serious business of his office lies in determining the size and composition of the strategic nuclear forces needed to prevent Soviet leaders from having any realistic expectation of gaining an exploitable military advantage and the general purpose forces appropriate to the initial defense of a small number of vital theaters in conjunction with allies.

It may prove clever tactically to present Congress with undisciplined budgets and let the members attempt to do the secretary's job, secure in the knowledge that they are not institutionally equipped to make hard and disciplined choices. It is by no means certain, however, that the responsible congressional committees will be able much longer to reconcile their desire for greater fiscal discipline with their propensity to chip away at the edges of the defense budget with a thousand minor cuts. Doomsayers are more often wrong than right, but the probability is on the increase that starting with the fiscal 1986 defense budget the long knives will be unsheathed and major surgery performed. Without cooperation from the defense department, damaging cuts could be made; with cooperation, cuts along with a balanced and healthy defense establishment, well able to fulfill its responsibilities, are still feasible.

Conclusion

Even if real growth in defense budget authority is limited to 3 percent during each of the next three fiscal years, instead of the 7.7 percent in the administration plan, and even if no major weapon system is canceled—with the exception of MX and a few other superfluous programs— it will still be possible to modernize existing forces, but at a slower and more prudent pace. What is more, a total of at least $78 billion in outlays can be saved, rather than the $27.7 billion proposed by the administration, during the next three fiscal years (table 19) and applied to the reduction of the federal deficit. Should Congress eventually become more willing to consider defense not as a latter-day WPA, but as the producer of a major public good that deserves scrutiny and control at least as careful as that accorded social security and medicaid, perhaps even more can be done. Perhaps extending programs can then be combined with canceling some of the Pentagon's more baroque fantasies; perhaps duplication and excessive pace can be traded for the capabilities that are most likely to be needed in the years ahead.

Dante may have had something resembling the Pentagon's budget in mind when he wrote, "Abandon all hope, ye who enter here." And the administration may yet find that Congress will once again heed the great poet's advice. There is still a chance, though, that the Senate and the House will finally turn for counsel to another source. It was Voltaire, who having noted that the English government ordered Admiral Byng to be shot for his failure to effect the relief of Minorca in 1756, wrote with admiration, "They think it a good idea in this country to shoot an admiral from time to time in order to encourage the others." Admirals and generals themselves no longer are fair game for such retribution, but there is very little reason why some of their ships, missiles, aircraft, and other appurtenances should not be. As the Marquise du Deffand remarked about the legend that St. Denis walked ten kilometers carrying his head in his hand, "the distance doesn't matter; it is only the first step that is difficult." It is still not too late to try the first step.